A Survey of Fiction

UNDERSTANDING LITERATURE

Janet M. Davis

American Guidance Service, Inc.
4201 Woodland Road
Circle Pines, MN 55014-1796
1-800-328-2560

ISBN 0-7854-2422-9

Product Number: 91550

A 0 9 8 7 6 5 4 5 3

Contents

Acknowledgments

From "The Adventure of the Speckled Band" from *The Complete Sherlock Holmes* by Sir Arthur Conan Doyle. Reprinted by permission.

From *Many Moons* by James Thurber. Copyright © 1943 by James Thurber. Copyright © renewed 1971 by Helen Thurber and Rosemary A. Thurber. Reprinted by arrangement with Rosemary A. Thurber and The Barbara Hogenson Agency. All rights reserved.

Unit 1
Literature

Lesson 1

How to Recognize Literature

Introduction

Literature includes **short stories, novels, plays,** and **poems.** Not all writings of these types are literature, however. Even though it is fun and interesting to read, much **popular fiction** is not literature.

Literature Identification

A main difference between literature and popular fiction is the purpose behind the writing. The purpose of popular fiction is to entertain. Most popular fiction tells a story that is clear and interesting. These light and fun writings are relatively easy to read. People usually choose to read popular fiction for relaxation and entertainment.

Literature can be entertaining, but it has other purposes as well. One purpose is to share the author's view of life. Literature is often about such large ideas such as truth, reality, and the meaning of life. Because literature tries to make people think about complex ideas, literature will often be deep itself. Readers are required to do more than relax and be entertained. They must also think and try to understand the author's ideas.

Literature can explore almost any subject matter. Along with the main topic, readers encounter many common experiences and emotions. Some examples of these common underlying themes include love and hate, violence and peace, wisdom and foolishness, and birth and death.

Literature Terms

literature

short story

novel

play

poem

popular fiction

A. Choose the best replacement for the bold words or phrases. Write the letter of your answer on the line

_____ 1. **Writing that has artistic value** can explore almost any subject.

_____ 2. Finding time to read **a tale told in a few pages** is easy.

_____ 3. **A book-length story** usually takes a while to read.

_____ 4. **Stories written to be acted out** include stage directions.

_____ 5. Fewer words are needed in **stories written in verse.**

_____ 6. **A story written just for fun** is usually read for relaxation and entertainment.

a. short story

b. novel

c. plays

d. poems

e. literature

f. popular fiction

B. Answer these questions with complete sentences.

1. What is the main difference between literature and popular fiction?

_____

_____

_____

2. What is one purpose of literature?

_____

_____

_____

3. What subject matter can literature explore? Give an example of a common theme in literature.

_____

_____

_____

Lesson 2

Why Study Literature?

Introduction

In *Walden,* American author Henry David Thoreau calls literature "golden words which the wisest men . . . have uttered" and "the noblest recorded thoughts of man." Why should we study literature?

Benefits of Studying Literature

By reading literature, we can learn what wise people think now or have thought in the past. We can read about experiences and emotions that are common to all of us. We do not have to agree with authors' ideas to gain from reading literature. Reading the ideas of others can cause us to think more clearly about our own ideas.

Literature gives us a chance to live through our imaginations. We can enjoy many things which we might not be able to do in real life. There is an old saying that "experience is the best teacher." This statement might be true, but people are not able to do everything that they would like to do. People have limits on time, energy, and money. Literature allows us to imagine ourselves living in different times and places. Literature also presents us with new ideas.

A. Answer these questions to get some ideas about how reading literature can make your world seem bigger and more interesting.

1. If you could visit any place in the world, where would you go?

   _____

2. If you could live in another time, when would you choose?

   _____

3. If you could have any job, where would you work?

   _____

4. If you could be any age, how old would you be?

   _____

B. Use your imagination as you read the summaries below. Place a check mark by any of the following situations that interest you. Try reading these books or stories.

_____ 1. How would it feel to love someone who was hated by your family?
Romeo and Juliet by William Shakespeare

_____ 2. How would it feel to discover a family's dark secret?
Jane Eyre by Charlotte Brontë

_____ 3. What was it like trying to survive in the South after the Civil War?
Gone With the Wind by Margaret Mitchell

_____ 4. How would it feel if your happiness came from a different direction than others thought it should?
Their Eyes Were Watching God by Zora Neale Hurston

_____ 5. What would it be like to be a ten-year-old who is marooned on an island with your classmates?
Lord of the Flies by William Golding

For Further Learning: Use your answers to Activities A and B to find books or stories that relate to your interests. Ask a librarian or use the Internet to help you search.

Unit 2
Basic Definitions

Lesson 1
Titles

Introduction

The title of a work of fiction is important. Two basic purposes of titles are:

- To capture the reader's interest
- To give the reader a clue about the author's direction

Types of Titles

Look closely at a title before you begin to read a story or poem. You can get an idea of what the author considers important. In general, there are four types of titles.

- The **place title** is used when the setting is important.

  Example: *Walden* by Henry David Thoreau

- The **name title** stresses a main character.

  Example: *Oliver Twist* by Charles Dickens

- The **plot title** calls attention to actions and events.

  Example: "To Build a Fire" by Jack London

- The **idea title** emphasizes theme.

  Example: "The Most Dangerous Game" by Richard Connell

A. Read each title below. For each, decide which elements you would expect to find stressed in that story. Write the correct letters on the lines.

_____ 1. *Romeo and Juliet*	**a.** setting
_____ 2. "To Build a Fire"	**b.** character
_____ 3. *A Tale of Two Cities*	**c.** plot
_____ 4. "The Most Dangerous Game"	**d.** idea

B. Answer these questions, using what you have learned about titles.

1. What are the two basic purposes of a title?

_____

_____

2. What does the title of a piece of literature tell you?

_____

_____

C. Write your own title for each of the types listed below. Be creative.

1. place title: _____

2. name title: _____

3. plot title: _____

4. idea title: _____

Lesson 2
Levels of Meaning

Introduction

Works of literature can have from one to five levels of meaning. The different points of view give readers more to think about. A story does not need all these levels to be interesting. However, one of the traits that make great works of literature stand out is that they often do offer all or most of the five levels. The descriptions below explain the different levels.

The Realistic Level

Realistic means "true-to-life." The realistic level is also called the literal level. A work of fiction must tell a story that readers believe. Even in a work of fantasy or science fiction, readers must believe that the events are possible.

To find the realistic level in a story, ask: "What happened?"

The Psychological Level

The study of human thoughts, feelings, and behavior is known as **psychology.** In fiction, readers often know much about a character's inner thoughts and feelings. Readers also might know why a character behaves in certain ways. The reasons for a person's behavior are called motivations.

To find the psychological level of a story, ask: (1) "Do I know the character's thoughts and feelings?" and (2) "Do I know the character's motivations?"

The Sociological Level

Groups in society usually have their own laws and customs. The study of groups and their laws and customs is called **sociology.** In some stories the laws and customs of the group have an effect upon the characters.

To find the sociological meaning in a story, ask: "Do the customs or laws of society affect the characters' actions or cause them problems?"

Literature Terms

realistic

psychology

sociology

symbols

universal

personal

functional

philosophy

The Symbolic Level

Words, pictures, and objects are all **symbols** that stand for something other than what they actually are. Some symbols are **universal:** they have the same meaning to almost everybody. For instance, a building with a red cross on the front is a sign of a place to go for medical care. Other symbols are **personal** or **functional.** They have meaning only to some people. For instance, if a boy always brings pink roses to a girl, a pink rose might become the symbol of joy in their relationship. If the relationship ends, a pink rose could then symbolize sadness.

To find the symbolic level, ask: "Are there any words, pictures, or objects in the story that stand for something other than what they are?"

The Philosophical Level

Philosophy includes thoughts and attitudes toward life. It includes feelings about what is important and about what is right and wrong. Philosophy has to do with attitudes about people, society, and the meaning of life. People's philosophies are their versions of the truth.

To find the philosophical level in a story, ask: (1) "What does the author seem to feel is true about life?" and (2) "What do the characters seem to feel is true about life?"

A. Choose the best replacement for the bold words or phrases. Write the letter of your answer on the line.

_____ 1. Words, pictures, and objects are **items that stand for something else.**

_____ 2. The **up front, or literal,** parts of a story do not include the deeper meanings.

_____ 3. **The study of people living together in groups** brings deep meaning to many stories.

_____ 4. **The way people think, feel, and behave** guides many story plots.

_____ 5. The girl's blanket had a value that was **meaningful only to her.**

_____ 6. **Basic ideas about life** come through in a person's actions.

_____ 7. The artist created a drawing that was **filling a specific need.**

_____ 8. Slang causes problems because it is not **understood the same by everybody.**

a. realistic
b. psychology
c. sociology
d. symbols
e. universal
f. personal
g. functional
h. philosophy

B. Match each level of meaning to the question you would ask to discover it.

_____ 1. Realistic

_____ 2. Psychological

_____ 3. Sociological

_____ 4. Symbolic

_____ 5. Philosophical

a. Do customs or laws affect the character's behavior?

b. What do the characters or the author think about life?

c. What happens in the story?

d. What are the motivations of the characters?

e. Does anything in the story (a word or a picture) stand for more than it actually is?

C. Read the statement. If the statement is true, write *True*. If it is false, write *False*.

_____ 1. Symbolic means "true-to-life."

_____ 2. Groups in society have their own customs and laws.

_____ 3. A work of literature can never have all five levels of meaning.

_____ 4. Reasons for a person's behavior are called motivations.

_____ 5. The psychological level reveals the character's thoughts and feelings.

_____ 6. Symbols can be universal or personal.

_____ 7. Meaning on the philosophical level is revealed by showing what an author feels about the meaning of life.

_____ 8. Sociology includes thoughts and attitudes toward life.

_____ 9. Psychology is the study of human thoughts, feelings, and behavior.

_____ 10. Universal symbols have different meanings to many different people.

Lesson 3

Types of Writing

Introduction

Like every subject of study, literature has its own special vocabulary. Knowing these special words makes it easier to read and talk about literature. Study the vocabulary definitions below.

Vocabulary

- **Fiction**—A story made up by the author

  Example: *The Wizard of Oz* is a fiction story.

- **Nonfiction**—Writing based on facts. A true story

  Example: Information about World War II that is included in a history book is nonfiction.

- **Prose**—Writing done in sentences and paragraphs

  Example: almost all novels and short stories are completely written in prose. Both *The Wizard of Oz* and information about World War II in a history book are written in prose.

- **Poetry**—Writing done in lines or stanzas (groups of lines)

  Example: "The Midnight Ride of Paul Revere" is poetry that was written in stanzas.

- **Narrative**—Writing that tells a story. It may be either prose or poetry

  Examples: *The Wizard of Oz,* information about World War II that is included in a history book, and "The Midnight Ride of Paul Revere" are all narratives.

- **Lyric**—Writing that creates an impression and a mental image or which expresses an emotion. Lyrics have a sense of melody about them.

  Example: Lyric poems are often used in songs. "America the Beautiful" is an example of a lyric poem that has been used in a song.

A. Choose the best replacement for the bold words or phrases. Write the letter of your answer on the line.

_____ 1. **Writing done in groups of lines** sometimes uses rhyming words.

_____ 2. Aunt Anne tells the best **made up** stories.

_____ 3. Clint sold his **words with the sense of melody** to the band.

_____ 4. Many **actual, true to life** stories become best sellers.

_____ 5. The **words that told the story** sounded oddly familiar.

_____ 6. **Writing done in sentences and paragraphs** is quite common.

a. poetry

b. fiction

c. nonfiction

d. lyrics

e. prose

f. narrative

B. Write two facts that relate to fiction and two that relate to nonfiction.

1. fiction

_____

_____

2. nonfiction

_____

_____

C. Read each of the following writing descriptions. Write *F* if the description is fiction or *N* if it is non-fiction.

_____ 1. A story about an imaginary journey

_____ 2. A news article about a robbery

_____ 3. A book explaining jet engines

_____ 4. A poem about a loved one's dream

_____ 5. An article on riding horses safely

_____ 6. A book about rabbits that speak

_____ 7. A book about a living person's life

_____ 8. An article about proper gardening

D. Read the passages below. Mark whether each passage is prose or poetry and narrative or lyric by putting check marks on the lines.

1. "I wandered lonely as a cloud
    That floats on high o'er vales and hills,
    When all at once I saw a crowd,
    A host, of golden daffodils,
    Beside the lake, beneath the trees,
    Fluttering and dancing in the breeze."

    — from "The Daffodils" by William Wordsworth

    a.   _____ prose

       OR

         _____ poetry

    b.   _____ narrative

       OR

         _____ lyric

2. Once upon a time, there was a tortoise who was challenged to a race by a rabbit. All the animals of the forest laughed because no one believed that the tortoise had a chance of winning such a race. The tortoise, however, accepted the challenge. He did not appear to be worried about the outcome.

    When the day for the race dawned, the tortoise arrived early at the starting line. The rabbit, meanwhile, had slept late. He was just finishing his breakfast when the starting gun went off.

    — paraphrase from Aesop's Fables

    a.   _____ prose

       OR

         _____ poetry

    b.   _____ narrative

       OR

         _____ lyric

Lesson 4

Genres

Introduction

Genre is a word that means "type" or "kind" When people speak about literary genres, they simply mean a type of literature.

The common genres of fiction are the short story, the novel, the play, and the narrative poem. Read an overview of each fiction genre below. As you read, keep in mind that there are no strict rules about what a work of fiction must be. Each author is free to create differences as desired. The explanations below provide a general and useful guide.

The Short Story

- Definition: A short story is short because it is not as long as a novel.
- Length: Short stories range from one or two pages to many pages. A short story does not have to be a definite length. However, it is usually short enough to be read all at one time.
- Parts: A short story will have at least one **character.** However, most short stories include more than one person or animal and some even have many characters. A short story also has a **setting** (time and place) and a **plot** (what happens in the story). To make the story interesting to read, a **conflict** of some sort is usually included. Often there will be a **theme** (the main idea)
- Purpose: The short story will, as its name suggests, tell a story. Short stories are meant to be read.

The Novel

- Definition: The novel is a story that fills an entire book.
- Length: Novels have no set length, but they are the longest form of fiction usually including well over 100 pages. Reading a novel might take several days.
- Parts: A novel will have characters, setting, plot, and conflict. Usually, it will have a theme. Novels usually have more characters and details than shorter forms of fiction. But, a novel could possibly have only one character. The plot of a novel will be more fully developed than in shorter fiction. Often, in addition to the main plot, there will be other, less important plots called **sub-plots.**
- Purpose: The novel will tell one or more stories. It is meant to be read.

Literature Terms

genre

character

setting

plot

conflict

theme

sub-plot

The Play

- Definition: A play is a story written in speaking parts for the different characters. Also included are a setting and descriptions of character movements.

- Length: The performance of some plays takes less than an hour while others take hours. Likewise, the written versions of plays vary quite a bit.

- Parts: A play has characters, a setting, and a plot

- Purpose: Like the other genres, a play tells a story. It is possible to read a play privately, just as one reads a short story or a novel. However, unlike other types of fiction, a play is meant to be performed out loud by a group. The members in the group each act out the part of a character. This format makes a play a fun, active experience.

The Narrative Poem

- Definition: A narrative poem is a story that is told in verses or stanzas (poetry). These verses or stanzas are the main difference between a narrative poem and a short story. The short story is written in sentences and paragraphs (prose).

- Length: Narrative poems have no set length, but they are usually longer than other poems. More words are needed to tell a whole story.

- Parts: A narrative poem will have one or more characters, a plot, and a setting. Conflict and a theme are also usually included.

- Purpose: Narrative poems tell a story and are meant to be read.

A. Choose the best replacement for the bold words or phrases. Write the letter of your answer on the line.

_____ 1. The **main idea of a story** might never be directly explained.

_____ 2. The **location and time for a story** could be on a hill at noon.

_____ 3. A story without a **problem or struggle** is not very interesting.

_____ 4. A story with a lot of **minor story lines** could be both interesting and confusing.

_____ 5. Some people would rather read certain fiction **types** than others.

_____ 6. In a good story, the **events in the story** keep the reader interested.

_____ 7. A **person or animal in a story** often seems very real.

a. genres

b. character

c. setting

d. plot

e. conflict

f. theme

g. sub-plots

B. Check your understanding of the explanations you have just read by completing the sentences below. Look back to the explanations for the correct words or phrases.

1. Genre means _____ .

2. The four common genres of fiction are: _____ , _____ ,

_____ , and _____ .

3. Unlike the short story and the novel, the play is meant to be _____ .

4. A narrative poem is a poem that tells a _____ .

5. All four of the common genres tell a _____ .

C. Think back to different stories you have read. Try to recall one example of each of the four common genres of fiction. List the titles below. If you have not read a certain genre, ask a librarian to suggest an example for you to read.

1. Short Story: _____

2. Novel: _____

3. Play: _____

4. Narrative Poem: _____

D. Which of the four genres do you enjoy (or think you would enjoy) the most? Explain your reasoning. Use complete sentences.

_____

_____

_____

_____

_____

_____

Lesson 5

Common Elements of Stories

Introduction

As you learned in Lesson 4, the common purpose of all genres of fiction is to tell a story. The basic building blocks of all stories are character, setting, and plot. It is impossible to have a story without these three elements.

Character

A character is a personality. Usually a character is either a human or an animal. A story may have one or more characters. Characters in fiction are usually imaginary people whom the author has created. Even though a character is imaginary, he or she must seem **believable** to the reader.

Sometimes an author will use **historical people** as characters. Historical people actually lived or are still living. Even with historical people, the author must imagine how the people would think, talk, or behave in certain situations.

To locate the characters in a story, ask: "Who are the personalities?"

Setting

The setting of a story tells where a story happens and when it takes place. These pieces of information are commonly called **place** and **time.**

The place in which a story happens may be specific or very general. A story that takes place in a house on Elm Street in Topeka, Kansas, is located specifically. A story that happens in an unnamed far-away land has a general place setting. The place setting can be a field, a road, a room, a house, a town, a car—any place where something can happen. The place can be real or imagined. The place setting might change during a story if the characters move from one location to another.

A story can take place in the past, the present, or the future. Everything that occurs must have already happened, be happening now, or be going to happen later. Just as with place, the time can be specific or general. The time setting can be as specific as on January 12, 1633, at 10:15 A.M., or it could be as general as "once upon a time." Time settings change when a story takes place over days, months, or years.

To determine the setting, ask: "Where does the story take place?" and "When does the story take place?"

Literature Terms

believable

historical people

place

time

structure

Plot

Plot is what happens in a story. It is the action in a story. Two important aspects of plot are conflict and **structure**.

Conflict is the struggle that occurs between a character and some other person, object, or force. It adds suspense and excitement to a story. Conflict can take many forms. A fist fight is physical conflict. Making a difficult decision is psychological conflict.

Structure is the planned order of the events of a story. Authors have many choices about how to plan stories. They can present events in the order in which they happened. They can present the facts in backward order, beginning with the most recent. They can begin in the middle of a story and fill in the background later. They can select events as they appear to one of the characters.

To find the plot of a story, ask:

"What happened?"

"With what conflicts do the characters struggle?"

"How do the characters deal with these conflicts?"

"In what arrangement or order do events occur?"

A. Choose the best replacement for the bold words or phrases. Write the letter of your answer on the line.

_____ 1. The **planned order of events** could be from past to present.	**a.**	believable
_____ 2. The **location where the story happens** is part of the setting.	**b.**	historical people
_____ 3. Readers like characters that are **true to the story**.	**c.**	place
_____ 4. Authors often model characters after **humans who are living**.	**d.**	time
_____ 5. Knowing the **hour, year, or century** makes a story more real.	**e.**	structure

B. Read the words listed below. Write each word under the correct story area.

structure   person   animal   time   conflict   place

Plot   **Character**   **Setting**

_____   _____   _____

_____   _____   _____

C. Match each item below to the correct story part. Write *C* for character, *S* for setting, or *P* for plot.

_____ **1.** a room in an old house

_____ **2.** a fight over food between two dogs

_____ **3.** February 2, 1955

_____ **4.** A man hides in an abandoned warehouse.

_____ **5.** Tom Sawyer

_____ **6.** Once upon a time . . .

_____ **7.** First, he caught a bus, then he . . .

_____ **8.** a teenage girl

_____ **9.** New York City

_____ **10.** He could not decide which girl he liked best.

_____ **11.** a lonely country road

_____ **12.** early in the morning

D. Choose one of your favorite stories. Use the facts from the story to complete the information below.

1. Title: _____

2. Main Characters: _____

3. Setting

    a. Place: _____

    b. Time: (Circle one)   Past   Present   Future

    Do events happen in time order?   yes   no

    Do events happen in backward order?   yes   no

    Do events happen in back and forth order?   yes   no

4. Identify one conflict in the story: _____

Mastery Lesson #1

A. Read the story "The Lady, or the Tiger?" by Frank Stockton. You will find it in Appendix A beginning on page 84.

B. Answer numbers 1–3 with examples from "The Lady, or the Tiger?" Then, decide if the story is literature or popular fiction.

   1. Literature makes people think.

     Example in story: _____

     _____

     _____

   2. Literature is often about large concepts.

     Example in story: _____

     _____

     _____

   3. Literature explores common experiences and emotions.

     Example in story: _____

     _____

     _____

   4. "The Lady, or the Tiger?" is _____

C. What type of title is "The Lady, or the Tiger?" Circle the correct answer. Then, on the lines, explain your choice.

   1. place title   name title   plot title   idea title

     _____

     _____

     _____

D. To read a story meaningfully, it is necessary to understand the plot on a realistic level. Test your understanding by circling the correct answers.

1. The king was only partly

   a. civilized.   **b.** weak.   **c.** pleased.

2. The accused person determined the outcome of the trial by opening

   a. a sealed envelope.   **b.** a secret ballot.   **c.** one of two doors.

3. When the accused person was decided to be guilty, he was

   a. put in prison.   **b.** eaten by a tiger.   **c.** hanged the next day.

4. When the accused person was decided to be innocent, he was

   a. sent home.   **b.** given an apology.   **c.** married to a lovely lady.

5. The princess hated

   a. the chosen girl.   **b.** her father.   **c.** the man who loved her.

6. Other than pure chance, the young man's only hope lay with

   a. the king.   **b.** the tiger.   **c.** the princess.

7. The princess gave a signal by

   a. screaming.   **b.** flashing a light.   **c.** raising her right hand.

8. The signal was seen by

   a. only the young man.   **b.** no one.   **c.** the entire crowd.

E. Use details from "The Lady, or the Tiger?" to complete the information below.

1. Title: _____

2. Main Characters: _____

   _____

3. Setting

   a. Place: _____

   b. Time: (Circle one)   Past   Present   Future

   Do events happen in time order?   yes   no

   Do events happen in backward order?   yes   no

   Do events happen in back and forth order?   yes   no

4. Identify one conflict in the story:

_____

F. Decide which level of meaning each of the following items represents. Write the correct letter on the line provided. Review pages 7–8 if necessary.

a. psychological   **b.** sociological   **c.** symbolic   **d.** philosophical

_____ **1.** The author presents the idea that the souls of lovers become one.

_____ **2.** The method of trial in this kingdom involves a tiger.

_____ **3.** The jealousy of the princess is described.

_____ **4.** The king believes that the minds of his people are refined by watching the trials.

_____ **5.** The tiger represents death. The lady represents life.

_____ **6.** It is forbidden for a common person to fall in love with the princess.

_____ **7.** The doors represent the unknown.

_____ **8.** The princess has horrible dreams.

_____ **9.** The king thinks the fairness of his method is obvious.

_____ **10.** The reader must decide the ending.

G. Use complete sentences to answer these questions.

  1. What is an emotion that you have felt in the past that was also experienced by a character in "The Lady, or the Tiger?" Name the emotion, the character in the story who experienced it, and explain how you have experienced it.

_____

_____

_____

  2. How does your idea of justice compare to the King's idea of justice in the story?

_____

_____

_____

  3. Imagine you could be one character from the story. Who would you be? How would you have felt about an "appointed day" in the arena?

_____

_____

_____

Unit 3
Character

Lesson 1

How Character is Developed: Appearance

Introduction

Characters, as you know, are the people or beings in stories. Sometimes they are animals that act like people. Usually, the more true-to-life the characters are, the more interesting the story. Most readers want to be able to form an idea of what the characters look like. **Mental pictures** help readers to think of characters as true-to-life people or animals.

Description

A **description** is a written sketch. The author describes the character's **appearance** in a direct way. The careful reader will pay close attention to the words that the author chooses to describe a character. A great many of these words will be **adjectives**. Adjectives are words that describe, such as *green, tall, hollow,* and *loud.* Sometimes authors will use comparisons to paint mental pictures for readers.

In the selection below, author Washington Irving describes Ichabod Crane. Ichabod is the main character of *The Legend of Sleepy Hollow.*

> He was tall, but exceedingly lank, with narrow shoulders, long arms and legs, hands that dangled a mile out of his sleeves, feet that might have served for shovels, and his whole frame most loosely hung together. His head was small, and flat on top, with huge ears, large green glassy eyes, a long snipe nose, so that it might have been mistaken for a weathercock perched upon his spindle neck, to tell which way the wind blew. To see him striding along the profile of a hill on a windy day, with his clothes bagging and fluttering about him, one might have mistaken him for the genius [image] of famine descending upon the earth, or some scarecrow eloped from a cornfield.

Literature Terms

mental picture

description

appearance

adjective

Vocabulary Help

lank—skinny

snipe—a bird with a long bill

spindle—a thin metal part that serves as an axis

famine—short on food

A. Choose the best replacement for the bold words or phrases. Write the letter of your answer on the line.

    _____ 1. Authors often describe characters' **face, hair, body shape, clothes, and ways of movement** in fairly complete detail.

    _____ 2. Authors use words like **tall, narrow, long, and flat** to help readers see the characters.

    _____ 3. It is hard for readers to see a character in their minds if no **written sketch** is given by the author.

    _____ 4. Authors tell what characters look like so readers can have **images in their heads** about each character.

    a. mental pictures

    b. appearance

    c. description

    d. adjectives

B. Washington Irving uses many adjectives to describe the various body parts of Ichabod Crane. List the adjectives that are used to describe Ichabod's parts. The author uses more than one adjective for some body parts. The first answer has been provided for you.

1. shoulders: <u>narrow</u>

2. arms and legs: _____

3. head: _____ _____

4. ears: _____

5. eyes: _____ _____ _____

6. nose: _____ _____

C. In several instances, Irving compares Ichabod (or some part of Ichabod) to something else. Fill in the blanks to complete these sentences.

1. Ichabod's feet look like _____ .

2. His head "might have been mistaken for a _____ ."

3. When he was walking on a windy day, Ichabod looked like the image of

_____ .

4. He also looked like a _____ from a cornfield.

D. Think about how the name Ichabod Crane fits his character. Answer the questions below with complete sentences.

    1. What are some words that you think of when you hear the name Ichabod?

      _____

      _____

      _____

    2. A crane is a kind of bird. Based on what you know about Ichabod, what kind of a bird do you think a crane is? Give reasons for your answer.

      _____

      _____

      _____

E. Draw a picture of Ichabod Crane. Use the description from Irving's story and your answers to the activities in this lesson as guides. Include as many details as possible.

Lesson 2

How Character is Developed: Personality

Introduction

More so than appearance, **personality** defines and explains real people. Understanding a person's personality lets us understand the person. Authors give personalities to characters to make them more real to readers.

Personality is more complicated than physical appearance and more difficult to see. Therefore, an author will use a variety of techniques to reveal the character's personality. The readers can learn about a character's personality from:

- What the author or narrator says about how the character thinks or behaves.

- What the character says, does, or thinks.

- What other characters say, do, or think about the character.

Let us look at each of these ways of **developing** a character's personality.

What the Author Says About the Character

In *The Legend of Sleepy Hollow,* the author Washington Irving tells us that Ichabod's heart yearned after the beautiful Katrina Van Tassel. Katrina happens to be the only daughter of the richest farmer in the area. Ichabod visits Katrina at her father's richly decorated home. The house sits in the middle of many acres of land. Ichabod has the following reaction:

> As the enraptured Ichabod fancied all this, and as he rolled his great green eyes over the fat meadow lands, the rich fields of wheat, of rye, of buckwheat, and Indian corn, and the orchard, his heart yearned after the damsel who was to inherit these domains, and his imagination expanded with the idea, how they might be readily turned into cash, and the money invested.

Literature Terms

personality

developing

straightforward

From this passage, readers can get a sense of greed flowing through Ichabod's blood. Although the author does not come right out and say that Ichabod is greedy, readers can pick the feeling up by reading between the lines. Authors will sometimes share details by being very **straightforward** with the information. Other times, readers will be led down a path that requires reading between the lines. The straightforward method requires less work on the part of the reader. On the other hand, reading between the lines tends to be more interesting because it involves the reader in the process.

What the Character Says, Does, or Thinks

Unlike the characters in many stories, Ichabod never speaks. We cannot make any judgments by what he says. However, we do see his actions and know many of his thoughts.

Ichabod's favorite book is about the history of witchcraft in New England. Sometimes he sits around a fire at night with other townspeople. He likes to tell and listen to ghost stories. At the end of such evenings, Ichabod must walk home alone through the woods. One such walk is described below.

> What fearful shapes and shadows beset his path, amidst the dim and ghostly glare of a snowy night! With what wistful look did he eye every trembling ray of light streaming across the waste field from some distant window! How often was he appalled by some shrub covered with snow, which like sheeted spectre beset his very path! How often did he shrink with curdling awe at the sound of his own steps on the frosty crust beneath his feet; and dread to look over his shoulder.

What Other Characters Say, Do, or Think About the Character

Ichabod has a frightful experience. He is chased by a headless man on horseback! Ichabod leaves the community very suddenly in the middle of the night. We learn that the people wonder if he has drowned, so they search the river for his body. They also gossip about his mysterious disappearance at church on Sunday. After that, "as he was a bachelor, and in nobody's debt, nobody troubled his head any more about him."

This situation makes it very clear just exactly how little the people of the community cared about Ichabod. The author Washington Irving could simply have told readers that the people in the community did not know nor care much for Ichabod. Also, he could have pointed out that, because of this, no no one worried too much about his disappearance. Rather than telling readers that Ichabod had not really become a part of the community, he shows readers this reality through his description.

Vocabulary Help

beset—filled; overcame

wistful—wanting; longing

appalled—shocked; filled with horror

spectre—ghost

curdling—increasing

awe—wonder

A. Choose the best replacement for the bold words or phrases. Write the letter of your answer on the line.

_____ 1. Once readers know **a character's typical patterns of behavior and thinking** they can guess what the character might do next.

_____ 2. Authors work at **creating the parts of** a character's nature.

_____ 3. Authors share some information in **direct** words.

a. personality

b. developing

c. straightforward

B. Show what you learned about Ichabod from his behavior and thoughts during the walk through the woods. If the statement is something you learned from the passage, write *True*. If you did not learn it from the passage, write *False*.

_____ 1. Ichabod is superstitious.

_____ 2. He does not believe in ghosts.

_____ 3. He has a powerful imagination.

_____ 4. His imagination has run away with him.

_____ 5. He is a sensible man.

_____ 6. Ichabod sees a bush covered by snow and thinks it is a ghost.

_____ 7. He is a very brave person.

_____ 8. His main emotion in this scene is happiness.

C. The author uses several words in this passage that create an atmosphere of fear. List five of them. One answer has been provided for you.

1. <u>ghostly</u>

2. _____

3. _____

4. _____

5. _____

D. We learn several things about Ichabod Crane from this passage. Read the sentence endings listed in the box below. Choose the correct ending to complete each sentence. Write each answer on the lines provided. The first answer has been done for you.

Sentence Endings

gossip at the church.	Katrina did not get married.
Ichabod was gone.	close friends in the community.
money to anyone.	impression on anyone in town.
if he drowned.	tell anyone that he was leaving.

Sentence Beginnings

1. He had not made a very great <u>impression on anyone in town.</u>

2. The people search to find out _____

3. Ichabod did not _____

4. Ichabod and _____

5. He did not owe _____

6. Ichabod seems to have had no _____

7. Nobody cared very much that _____

8. Ichabod's disappearance is the subject of _____

E. Review your knowledge of character. Write your answer to the question on the lines provided.

1. In what three different ways can readers learn about a character's personality?

_____

_____

_____

For Further Learning: Read *The Legend of Sleepy Hollow* by Washington Irving to find out what ghostly happenings caused the mysterious disappearance of Ichabod Crane.

Lesson 3

Types of Characters: Flat and Round

Introduction

Types of characters vary as much as types of people. To make it easier for us to talk about characters in stories, certain terms are used. These words have special meanings when they are applied to characters in fiction. Two useful terms to apply to characters are **flat** and **round**.

Flat

A flat view of an object shows us only the surface from one side or from one angle. Imagine looking down on the flat surface of a can of peaches so that you can see only the top. If you are looking from an angle directly above the can, all that you will see is the flat top. If that were your only view of the can, you would know that the can is made of shiny metal. You would also know that the top has the shape of a circle.

With only this top view, you might make the mistake of thinking that the can is a flat object. You would not know about the bottom of the can. You would not know about the pictures and words on the sides of the can. You would not know about the contents of the can. In this same way, a character who is described from one angle is not known well by readers.

Round

A round view of an object shows us more angles. If we take the can of peaches and hold it differently, we are able to see more. We can see the shiny top. Some of the pictures and the words on the side show. The roundness of the can becomes clear. If we take a can opener and pry up the lid, we can see that the can has peaches inside. By tilting the can slightly, we can see the bottom of the can.

When we view the can from different angles, we get a more complete and accurate picture. Likewise, we can view characters from many angles.

Literature Terms

flat

round

relative

Relative Terms

When talking about characters, flat and round are **relative.** The roundest character in one story might seem flat in another story. This change of status happens because the amount of character description changes from story to story.

The words more and most are useful in comparing characters. A character will be more flat or more round than other characters in a story. The character in a story that you know least about is the flattest character. The character that you know most about is the roundest character.

Readers can know characters from a number of angles. These six categories are examples of information authors give about characters: appearance, likes, dislikes, attitude and behavior, goals or ambitions, and fears. A character who has been developed a little in each category is more rounded than a character who has been developed a lot from only a couple of angles.

The more round a character is, the better readers will feel they know that character. With characters (as with real people) physical appearance is only one aspect of the person. Likes and dislikes, feelings, behavior, dreams, concerns, and activities all contribute to an individual's personality.

The characters that are most flat will often be minor characters in a story. Usually, the character that is most round will be the main character in a story. Other characters will be more or less round depending upon how much the author reveals about them.

A. Choose the best replacement for the bold words or phrases. Write the letter of your answer on the line.

_____ 1. How well readers know a character is **based on the other characters.**   a. flat

_____ 2. Readers feel like they know characters who are **described in detail.**   b. round

_____ 3. **Vaguely described** characters are easy to forget.   c. relative

B. Read each statement. If the statement is true, write *True.* If it is false, write *False.*

_____ 1. A character who has been developed in all six categories is usually very flat.

_____ 2. Readers know quite a bit about the personalities of round characters.

_____ 3. The main character in a story is usually flat.

_____ 4. By the end of the story, the reader will know round characters better than flat ones.

_____ 5. The terms round and flat apply only to a character's appearance.

C. Below is a list of characters along with information about each. Arrange the characters in order from most flat to most round. Give a #1 to the most flat character. Give a #5 to the most round character. (Hint: Do not be fooled by the number of words. Check to see how much you know about each character's personality.)

_____ 1. Joanna: plays drums in the high school band; eats health food; plays soccer; is afraid of thunderstorms

_____ 2. Carlos: young, sells newspapers on a street corner; is often teased about his freckles; smiles often; saves his money

_____ 3. Emily: very tall; has black hair; wears glasses and a lot of jewelry

_____ 4. Mark: 55 years old; collects stamps; is proud of his two children; worries about his sick wife; gives money to charity

_____ 5. Sankri: has short hair; works at a bank; is always in a hurry

D. Susan is 16 years old. That is all we know about her. Therefore, she is a very flat character. To turn Susan into a round character, add information in each of the categories below. The more specific you are, the more round Susan will become. Be creative!

Appearance: _____

Likes: _____

Dislikes: _____

Attitude and behavior: _____

Goals or dreams: _____

Fears: _____

Lesson 4

Types of Characters: Static and Dynamic

Introduction

Characters' inner selves are either **static** or **dynamic**. People's inner selves are made up of their beliefs, values, and attitudes. Their outlooks on life and their behaviors will be based upon these **internal** beliefs, values, and attitudes. Internal beliefs that never change are static. Those that change are dynamic.

The words static and dynamic are most useful in describing a main character because more information is given about a main character than about a minor character.

Static

Static characters are unchanging. They do not grow internally. This lack of growth does not mean they are not growing taller or heavier. Height and weight are **external** growth factors. Static characters are those who do not grow internally. Their experiences in life do not cause their beliefs, values, and attitudes to change.

In some stories, many things happen to the characters without producing any real changes in their beliefs, values, or attitudes. Similar situations may exist in real life. We do many things and have many events happen to us that do not change our inner selves. A character who shows no significant internal change is a static character.

Dynamic

Dynamic characters grow and change because of their experiences. Again, this growth has nothing to do with externally growing taller or heavier. In stories, as in life, there are some events or forces that cause people to change internally. Their beliefs, values, and attitudes become different as a result of some event which causes them to see life differently. A character who shows a significant change in beliefs, values, and attitudes is dynamic.

Static or Dynamic?

Both static and dynamic characters are found in stories. Both types of characters can be interesting and true-to-life. Neither type is better than the other. Knowing the difference between the two adds to a reader's ability to understand a story.

Use the formula on the next page to decide if a character is static or dynamic.

Literature Terms

static

dynamic

internal

external

Step 1. List all known facts about the character's inner self early in the story. That is, list everything that is written about the character's beliefs, values, and attitudes.

Step 2. List all events that happen to the character and all the things the character learns throughout the story.

Step 3. List everything given about the character's inner self at the end of the story.

Step 4. Compare lists 1 and 3.

    a. If lists 1 and 3 are the same, or nearly the same, the person is static. Events that happened and things that were learned did not change the character's inner self.

    b. If lists 1 and 3 are different, the character is dynamic. The events of the story have caused the person's beliefs, values, and attitudes to change.

    c. Some characters are more dynamic than others. More differences between lists one and three show more dynamic characters.

The simple story below has two different endings. Read the beginning of the story and then both endings given on the next page. Depending on the ending, Rick is either a static or dynamic character.

Beginning

Rick is a high school senior. He is a poor student with few friends. In the beginning of the year, Rick hates school and wants to quit. As the year progresses, he makes friends with Tom.

Tom persuades Rick to try out for the basketball team. Rick makes the team. He gets along well with his coach and teammates.

After a few weeks, the coach tells Rick that he is a very valuable team member. All is going well until mid-term grades come out. Rick's name is on the warning list. The coach tells Rick to bring his grades up so he can stay on the team. Rick yells in response, "I don't need your worthless team. I don't need this stinking school." Then, he throws his basketball jersey on the gym floor and storms out of the gym and goes home.

On the way home, Rick bumped into Hank. Rick had met Hank about five years earlier, when Hank helped Rick's family move. "What's up, Rick? Why aren't you at school?" Hank asked.

Rick responded, "I'm quitting."

"Don't do that. I sure wish I hadn't quit. My back is giving me so much trouble that I can't work as a furniture mover anymore and I have no other skills."

First Ending

Rick listens to Hank. Later at home, Rick thinks all night long about his future. Rick decides to give school another chance. The next day he apologizes to the coach. The coach agrees to help find a tutor so Rick can get his grades up.

Rick also goes to his teachers for extra help. Some of his teammates form a study group. Rick's grades go up and he has a great basketball season.

In May, Rick graduates from high school. In the last scene of the story, we see him laughing and joking with his friends from the team. One of them asks him if he plans to go to college in the fall. Rick's answer is, "Maybe I will."

Second Ending

Rick is rude to Hank and tells him to leave him alone. Then he goes home. As the night goes on, he becomes angrier and angrier at the coach. He resents the school for having rules. He feels sorry for himself because he was not born a good student.

The next morning, Rick goes to the guidance counselor and tells her that he wants to quit school. She offers to arrange for him to get extra help from his teachers. Rick says, "No." He signs the withdrawal form. The counselor says that he must turn in his textbooks and basketball jersey. He gets his books from his locker and his jersey from the locker room.

As the story ends, we see Rick standing near the gym door. He is looking through the door at the basketball team. They call to him to come to practice. Rick turns and goes out of the school building. As he passes a waste basket, he pitches in his textbooks and basketball jersey.

Finally, he walks away—alone.

A. Circle the correct answer.

1. In the first ending, Rick is a (static, dynamic) character.

2. In the second ending, Rick is a (static, dynamic) character.

B. Choose the best replacement for the bold words or phrases. Write the letter of your answer on the line.

_____ 1. Most people undergo **inner** changes

_____ 2. **Never changing** characters are not very realistic.

_____ 3. Characters who are **changed by experiences in life** are true to life.

_____ 4. Growing taller is an example of a **physical body** change.

a. static

b. dynamic

c. internal

d. external

C. Certain events in this story affected Rick's attitude. Write *Yes* or *No* to show whether or not each event below probably affected his attitude.

_____ 1. Rick met a friend, Tom.

_____ 2. School work was hard for Rick.

_____ 3. Rick is a senior.

_____ 4. Rick talked with Hank.

_____ 5. Rick joined the basketball team.

_____ 6. Rick liked his coach.

_____ 7. Rick's family moved five years ago.

_____ 8. Rick became angry at the coach.

_____ 9. Rick liked being on the team.

_____ 10. Rick was a valuable team member.

D. Choose a story that you know well. Select a main character and complete the information below.

1. Title of Story: _____

2. Main Character: _____

3. Character's beliefs, values, and attitudes at the beginning of the story:

   _____

   _____

4. Things character experiences and learns during the story:

   _____

   _____

5. Character's beliefs, values, and attitudes at the end of the story:

   _____

   _____

6. Is the character static or dynamic? _____

Lesson 5

Hero or Protagonist? Antagonist or Foil?

Introduction

The **hero** is the central or most important character in a work of fiction. The hero can be male or female. In literature, if the central character is female, she is often called the **heroine.**

The Classical Hero

Our ideas about what a hero should be began with the ancient Greeks. We still read about the Greek heroes in famous stories such as *The Iliad, The Odyssey,* and stories about Theseus and Hercules.

These Greek heroes are called **classical heroes** or traditional heroes. The classical hero was used as a model for heroes for hundreds of years. Shakespeare's heroes, for example, are classical heroes. So is King Arthur. This kind of hero has certain characteristics.

- He is of noble birth. His father is usually a king or a person of very high rank. Sometimes, in the Greek stories, the hero's father is even a god.

- He is physically strong. Many of the Greek heroes had more strength than any real person could have. Hercules, for instance, could change the course of rivers. Atlas, another Greek hero, could hold the entire world on his shoulders. Sometimes the hero also had outstanding intelligence. Odysseus, for instance, could always outsmart his enemies.

- He has a great amount of self-confidence and faith in his own abilities.

- He has enormous amounts of courage.

- He is very independent. He often fights great battles alone. He also often ignores the advice of other people.

- He usually has to fight a series of evil characters or sometimes monsters to reach his goal.

- He often has a tragic **flaw.** The classical hero who is imperfect in some sad way is sometimes called a **tragic hero.** The tragic hero has a defect in his personality. Perhaps he is too proud or too ambitious. Perhaps he does not control his temper. Whatever his flaw is, it will bring him defeat.

- He is courageous and noble, even if he is defeated.

Literature Terms

hero

heroine

classical hero

flaw

tragic hero

protagonist

antagonist

foil

The Modern Hero

Some modern stories have classical heroes. However, as people came to believe in democracy and in the equality of all people, other kinds of heroes developed. Readers became interested in all sorts of people, not just people of noble birth.

In a modern story, the main character can be a man, a woman, or an animal. The person may be a farmer, a salesperson, a teacher, or a servant. The person may even be a murderer or a gangster. The word *hero* suggests someone who has mostly good qualities. Since the main character in modern stories is not required to have good qualities (although often does), a new word was needed to describe the main character. That word is **protagonist.**

The protagonist simply means the main character in the story. Whether the main character is male, female, or animal, the same term is used. Whether he or she is noble and good or lowly and wicked, the main character is still called the protagonist. All stories have this main character, a protagonist.

The **antagonist** is a character who opposes the main character in a story. If the main character is a detective, the antagonist might be a criminal. If the main character is a criminal, the antagonist might be the detective. Not all stories have an antagonist. If there is no character who opposes the main character, there is no antagonist.

Some stories also have a **foil.** This character causes problems for the main character by providing a contrast. Often, the foil is a friend of the main character.

To emphasize the physical strength of the main character, the author might contrast the individual with a weak character. To make fairness stand out in a character, a dishonest person could be used for comparison. This contrasting character is called a foil.

For example, Dr. Watson is a foil for Sherlock Holmes. Holmes is very intelligent and frequently has to explain things to Dr. Watson. Although Dr. Watson is not unintelligent, his slowness to understand emphasizes the special intelligence of Sherlock Holmes.

Not all stories have a foil.

A. Choose the best replacement for the bold words or phrases. Write the letter of your answer on the line.

_____ 1. Many stories have a **female main character**.

_____ 2. The **strong, courageous, noble-born hero** is no longer found in every story.

_____ 3. The main character's **imperfect trait** led to his defeat.

_____ 4. Many stories have a **male main character**.

_____ 5. The **main character who is wonderful and yet imperfect in some way** always ends up in self-defeat.

_____ 6. The **main character's enemy** can be good or evil.

_____ 7. A **character who has opposite traits** makes a main character's traits more obvious.

_____ 8. A **main character who is male or female** can be good or evil.

a. hero

b. heroine

c. classical hero

d. flaw

e. tragic hero

f. protagonist

g. antagonist

h. foil

B. Suppose that each character below has a quality that you want to emphasize. What quality would you give a foil to make a contrasting character? Write your answers on the lines provided.

1. Arturo is physically strong. His foil is _____ .

2. Mrs. Murray is very quiet. Her foil is _____ .

3. Joel is a good athlete. His foil is _____ .

4. Lisi is very intellectual. Her foil is _____ .

5. Satish is very tall and thin. His foil is _____ .

6. Emily is very serious about life. Her foil is _____ .

7. Trang is very shy. His foil is _____ .

8. Mr. Sechelski is a responsible person. His foil is _____ .

C. Read the two summaries below. In each case, decide which character is the protagonist, the antagonist, and the foil. Then, write the names of the correct characters on the lines provided.

1. The novel *Oliver Twist* by Charles Dickens is about a poor but honest young orphan named Oliver. Oliver is befriended by a young pickpocket, who is called The Artful Dodger. He gives Oliver food. He also takes Oliver to meet the gang of pickpockets with whom he lives. As the story progresses, a man named Bill Sikes is afraid that Oliver will give away the pickpockets' hiding place. Bill plans to murder Oliver.

   a. protagonist: _____

   b. antagonist: _____

   c. foil: _____

2. In the play *Macbeth,* by William Shakespeare, Macbeth is a noble. He is also very ambitious. He has a friend, also a noble, named Banquo. Macbeth and Banquo meet three witches who tell Macbeth that he will become king. They tell Banquo that his descendants will become kings. Macbeth's ambitions are aroused, and he plans to overthrow the existing king. Banquo, however, remains loyal to the king. Another noble named Macduff forms an army to fight Macbeth in his attempt to gain the throne.

   a. protagonist: _____

   b. antagonist: _____

   c. foil: _____

D. Test your understanding of the characteristics of the classical hero. Read the sentence endings given in the box below. Choose the appropriate ending to complete each sentence. Write the correct sentence endings on the lines provided.

Sentence Endings

in his own abilities.	a king, a god, or a person of high rank.
a tragic flaw.	to use would be heroine.
the advice of other people.	physical strength.
the traditional hero.	remains courageous and noble.
used as a model for hundreds of years.	a series of evil characters or monsters.

Sentence Beginnings

1. The classical hero is sometimes called

   _____

2. To be of noble birth means to be the son or daughter of

   _____

3. Sometimes the hero has great intelligence in addition to outstanding

   _____

4. The hero has a great amount of self-confidence and belief

   _____

5. The hero is sometimes so independent that he fights battles alone and ignores

   _____

6. In order to reach his goal, the hero usually has to fight

   _____

7. A tragic hero has a personality defect, called

   _____

8. Even if he is defeated, the classical hero

   _____

9. The classical hero was

   _____

10. If the classical hero were a woman, the appropriate word

   _____

Unit 4
Setting

Lesson 1

Place

Introduction

Every story happens in one or more places. Where a story happens is part of the story's setting. Sometimes the setting includes an actual place that the reader can locate on a map. Sometimes it is a place that the author has imagined. A story might happen in one place or several places. Often there is a main location that is the most important place.

Purpose of Setting

The place where a story happens can serve to make the story more realistic, set a mood or atmosphere, or help the plot.

Understanding the setting helps the reader to get more out of a reading experience. Stories are more realistic for readers when they can mentally form detailed picture. Read the following story settings and think about the different levels of settings.

- The child is sitting outside.

- The child is on a rock ledge at the zoo.

- The child is on a rock ledge inside a tiger's cage at the zoo.

The first setting results in a vague picture. The second setting allows the reader to create a mental picture. Putting the child on a rock ledge inside a tiger's cage adds a feel for the mood of the story. When a zoo worker and a tiger see the child at the same moment, the setting becomes very involved with the plot.

As these three settings show, knowing where a story happens helps readers understand the character's lives, the action of the plot, and the ideas of the author. Story location includes these main parts: geographical location, scenery, and arrangement of objects.

Literature Terms

specific

general

scenery

Geographical Location

Geographic location may be **specific** or **general**. Specific geographical locations are place names:

• Italy

• London

• Paris

• San Francisco

Examples of general locations are more broad:

• in a big city

• on a country road

Authors sometimes include both a specific and a general location:

• on a quiet street on the north side of Atlanta

Scenery

Scenery provides a physical background for a story. This background includes natural items such as mountains, skies, and rivers. Scenery also includes objects such as houses, rooms, and city streets. Knowing the scenery that surrounds a story lets readers develop a more complete mental picture.

Take the little boy in the tiger's cage. Add some scenery such as a gentle waterfall on a nice day. Now, readers can sense what might have attracted the child to the tiger's cage. Readers can picture a young boy on a rock ledge with his feet dangling in the pool of water.

Physical Arrangement of Objects

The physical arrangement of objects is very important to the plot of some stories. How the windows are placed in a room, where an open letter is lying, even the color of a tablecloth might affect how the story turns out. Physical placement is often especially important in mystery and detective stories. Imagine a zoo worker's ladder outside the tiger's cage. Readers can see how the child got into the cage.

In most stories, the setting is partly described near the beginning of the story. Then, the author adds details throughout the story. To understand the complete setting, you must read the entire story. Two partial descriptions of settings follow. As you read the descriptions, create a mental picture of the setting. Also, think about how the setting relates to the story.

"The Adventure of the Speckled Band"

"The Adventure of the Speckled Band," by Arthur Conan Doyle, concerns the famous detective Sherlock Holmes. He has been hired by Miss Stoner to investigate the mysterious death of her sister. That sister died in her locked bedroom from unknown causes. Miss Stoner is afraid for her own life. We learn early in the story that Miss Stoner lives with her stepfather in an old house in the English countryside. In the passage given below, Miss Stoner is showing Holmes the room in which her sister died. Miss Stoner is now sleeping in this room while her own bedroom is being remodeled.

In almost all stories, the setting makes the story seem more realistic. In "The Adventure of the Speckled Band," the setting helps the plot develop.

> It was a homely little room, with a low ceiling and a gaping fireplace, after the fashion of old country-houses. A brown chest of drawers stood in one corner, a narrow white-counterpaned bed in another, and a dressing-table on the left-hand side of the window. These articles, with two small wicker-work chairs, made up all the furniture in the room, save for a square of Wilton carpet in the center. The boards round and the paneling of the walls were of brown, worm-eaten oak, so old and discolored that it may have dated from the original building of the house. Holmes drew one of the chairs into a corner and sat silent, while his eyes traveled round and round and up and down, taking in every detail of the apartment.
>
> "Where does that bell communicate with?" he asked, at last, pointing to a thick bell-rope which hung down beside the bed, the tassel actually lying upon the pillow.
>
> "It goes to the housekeeper's room."
>
> "It looks newer than the other things."
>
> "Yes, it was only put there a couple of years ago."
>
> "Your sister asked for it, I suppose?"
>
> "No, I never heard of her using it. We used always to get what we wanted for ourselves. . . .
>
> "Why, it's a dummy," said he.
>
> "Won't it ring?"

(continued on the next page)

Vocabulary Help

homely—plain, simple

counterpaned—painted with colored stripes

wicker-work—basket-like, weaving done with dried plant stems

dummy—fake

ventilator—fresh air screen

singular—strange, stand out as odd

"No, it is not even attached to a wire. This is very interesting. You can see now that it is fastened to a hook just above where the little opening for the ventilator is."

"How very absurd! I never noticed that before."

"Very strange!" muttered Holmes, pulling at the rope. "There are two very singular points about this room. For example, what a fool a builder must be to open a ventilator into another room, when, with the same trouble, he might have communicated with the outside air!"

"That is also quite modern," said the lady.

"Done about the same time as the bell-rope?" remarked Holmes.

"Yes, there were several little changes carried out about that time."

"They seem to have been of a most interesting character— dummy bell-ropes, and ventilators which do not ventilate."

"The Monkey's Paw"

In "The Monkey's Paw" by W.W. Jacobs, an old man and his wife are given a dried monkey's paw. They are told that if they use the paw to make three wishes, the wishes will be granted. They are also warned that the paw is evil. They are advised to burn it instead of using it to make wishes. They do not follow this good advice. In the scene below, the old man has just made his third and last wish. Notice how the setting helps to set the story's mood.

> The knocking ceased suddenly, although the echoes of it were still in the house. He heard the chair drawn back, and the door opened. A cold wind rushed up the staircase, and a long loud wail of disappointment and misery from his wife gave him courage to run down to her side and then to the gate beyond. The street lamp flickering opposite shone on a quiet and deserted road.

A. Choose the best replacement for the bold words or phrases. Write the letter of your answer on the line.

_____ 1. A clearing in a cool forest is an example of an **inexact** place for a setting.

_____ 2. The Rotunda in the capitol building in Madison, Wisconsin, is an example of an **exact** place for a setting.

_____ 3. A barnyard and an orchard full of trees are examples of **background items** that could complete a setting.

a. specific

b. general

c. scenery

B. Adjectives are words that describe. They are very important in making the setting seem real. Read the sentences below from "The Adventure of the Speckled Band." Circle the adjectives the author used. The first one is done for you.

1. The room had a (low) ceiling.

2. It also had a gaping fireplace.

3. Among the furniture was a brown chest of drawers.

4. There was also a narrow white-counterpaned bed.

5. The furniture also included a rug and two small wicker-work chairs.

6. The paneling on the walls was of brown, worm-eaten oak.

7. The oak was old and discolored.

8. The bell-rope and the ventilator were new and more modern than anything else in the room.

C. Careful choice of words and details help to set a mood or atmosphere. The word *misery,* found in the passage from "The Monkey's Paw," is part of the mood of this passage. Write three more words that suggest the mood created by the setting.

_____

_____

_____

D. Use your creativity to decide upon a setting to go with each mood below. The first answer has been done for you.

1. terror

   <u>a person following you in the dark</u>

2. romance

   _____

   _____

3. nervousness

   _____

   _____

4. adventure

   _____

   _____

Lesson 2

Time

Introduction

A story must take place in a certain time—the past, the present, or the future. The time in which a story occurs is part of the story's setting.

Time Clues

Sometimes authors are very specific about time. They might even give exact dates if they are important to their stories. Often, however, it is not necessary to know the exact date to understand a story. Sometimes it is only necessary to know the general time period in which the story is set.

Sometimes authors tell the time periods. More often, authors give clues about the time. They assume that readers have some general history knowledge that will help them to understand the clues. If readers cannot follow the clues, it is easy to find the needed information in encyclopedias, in history books, or on the Internet.

For instance, the author might mention the following clues about time:

- historical events: World War II, the discovery of America, the invention of the automobile

- actual people: King Charles I, Pocahontas, Elvis Presley, Eleanor Roosevelt, George Bush

- styles of dress: miniskirts, buckskin trousers, tricorn hats, hoop skirts, bell bottoms, cargo pants

- methods of transportation: horses and buggies, steamboats, propeller airplanes, automobiles, jet planes

Clue Search

To figure the time setting of stories, it is important to pay attention to authors' clues. These clues may be scattered throughout a story. Sometimes it is necessary to do research in other books to figure out the approximate date during which a story took place.

A Tale of Two Cities

In some stories, the characteristics of the time are more important than the actual date. Below is the beginning paragraph of *A Tale of Two Cities*, a novel by Charles Dickens. Read it carefully to see the time in which this story takes place.

> It was the best of times, it was the worst of times, it was the age of wisdom, it was the age of foolishness, it was the epoch of belief, it was the epoch of incredulity, it was the season of Light, it was the season of Darkness, it was the spring of hope, it was the winter of despair, we had everything before us, we had nothing before us, we were all going direct to Heaven, we were all going direct the other way . . .

Dickens makes the point that the age he describes is an age of contrasts. Antonyms are words that are opposite in meaning. They are often used to show contrasts.

Dickens later tells the reader that the time of which he writes is the year 1775. He gives the date, however, only after he has emphasized the important characteristics of the age. This period of the French Revolution brought about the revolt of the people against the monarchy in France.

A. Choose the best replacement for the bold words or phrases. Write the letter of your answer on the line.

_____ 1. You are reading this sentence in the **point in time that is happening right now.**

_____ 2. Events that happened yesterday are taking place in the **point in time that has already gone by.**

_____ 3. No one knows what will happen in the **point in time that has not yet come.**

a. past
b. present
c. future

B. Use an encyclopedia, a history book, or the Internet to complete this activity. Find the time period in which the following events occurred. Write the year or years on the lines provided. The first example has been done for you.

1. _1789_____ Beginning of the French Revolution

2. _____ The presidency of George Washington

3. _____ The Civil War in the United States

4. _____ D-Day

5. _____ The fall of Rome

6. _____ The reign of Queen Victoria

C. Determine which type of time clue each of the following items is. Write the correct letter for each clue on the line.

_____ 1. Long dresses with hoops and petticoats

_____ 2. Pilgrims

_____ 3. Spacecraft

_____ 4. World War I

_____ 5. Landing on the moon

_____ 6. Knights in armor

_____ 7. Jet airplanes

a. historical event

b. actual people

c. style of dress

d. method of transportation

D. Reread the passage from *A Tale of Two Cities*. Match each word with its antonym, or opposite. Write the letter of the correct antonym on the line.

_____ 1. light

_____ 2. hope

_____ 3. belief

_____ 4. best

_____ 5. everything

_____ 6. wisdom

_____ 7. heaven

a. nothing

b. the other way

c. dark

d. foolishness

e. worst

f. despair

g. incredulity

Mastery Lesson#2

A. Read or review the story "The Lady, or the Tiger?" by Frank Stockton. You will find it in Appendix A beginning on page 84.

B. The two main characters of this story are the princess and the young man who is on trial for loving her. They are described in great detail. Read the adjectives listed in the box below. Write each adjective under the character it describes.

blooming	brave	handsome	fervent
tall	semi-barbaric	fair	hot-blooded
imperious	grand	anxious	intense

The Princess

_____

_____

_____

_____

_____

The Young Man

_____

_____

_____

_____

_____

C. Look at the two lists you have just created in Activity B above. Choose the correct answers to complete the following two statements.

_____ 1. The adjectives which refer to the young man mostly describe his

    a. appearance

    b. personality

_____ 2. The adjectives which refer to the princess mostly describe her

    a. appearance

    b. personality

D. Read the list of characters below. Arrange these characters in order from the most flat to the most round. Label the most flat character #1. Label the most round character #5.

_____ 1. the king

_____ 2. the princess

_____ 3. the young man

_____ 4. the people in the crowd

_____ 5. the lady behind the door

E. Circle the word or phrase in parentheses that most correctly completes each statement.

1. The princess is probably the best choice for the (protagonist, foil) in the story because the reader knows about the workings of her mind.

2. Some people, however, would argue that the main character is the (tiger, young man).

3. The lady behind the door serves as a (protagonist, foil) to the princess.

4. The ending of the story could make a difference. However, as the story stands, the characters are all (static, dynamic) because we do not see them change.

5. The young man, who is not of noble birth, (is, is not) presented as a classical hero.

6. In personality, the princess is portrayed as being very much like (her father, the young man).

F. We are told that the story takes place in "the very olden time." Some of the statements below suggest a very olden time. Others could just as likely take place in any time period. Write *Yes* beside each item that suggests a very olden time. Write *No* beside each item that could take place in any time period.

_____ 1. A tiger is used as a means of punishment.

_____ 2. Jealousy is felt toward a rival.

_____ 3. The word barbaric is used frequently.

_____ 4. Executions take place in front of a crowd.

_____ 5. A young man has to make a tough decision.

_____ 6. The rooms are curtained with skins.

_____ 7. Dying gladiators are mentioned.

_____ 8. It is a crime punishable by death for a common person to love a princess.

_____ 9. People gather in an arena to watch an event.

_____ 10. A father disapproves of his daughter's boyfriend.

G. Part of the setting of a story is the mood that the author creates. An author creates a particular mood by the choice of words and details. What is the mood of the story "The Lady, or the Tiger?" What words or details in the story help to create this mood?

1. Mood: _____

2. Words or Details: _____

_____

Unit 5
Plot

Lesson 1
Conflict

Introduction

Plot is what happens in a story. It is a planned series of actions that relate to one another. Plot always involves a conflict of some sort.

Conflict is a struggle between two opposing forces. One of those forces will usually be the main character, the protagonist. The interest of the story lies in seeing how the characters resolve the conflict.

Several types of conflict can exist in stories, just as they exist in life. Most stories present more than one type of conflict. The standard types of conflict are:

- Person versus person
- Person versus **society**
- Person versus self
- Person versus **nature**
- Person versus **fate**

The word person, as it is used here, means any protagonist in a story. That protagonist can be a man, woman, or animal. Protagonists' conflicts can be with another person, society, oneself, nature, or fate.

Person Versus Person

Person versus person means protagonist against antagonist. In this type of conflict, the main character will struggle against another character, an antagonist. This antagonist can be human or animal. Any story with a hero versus a **villain** is an example of person-versus-person conflict.

Literature Terms

society

nature

fate

villain

Person Versus Society

Person versus society means one protagonist against a community of people. In a story with this type of conflict, the protagonist will come into conflict with the laws, customs, or attitudes of a group of people.

Examples of this type of conflict include the woman who fights to change laws that she thinks are unjust, the student who does not accept school rules, or the man who tries to change public thinking on an issue.

Person Versus Self

Person versus self means that the protagonist is divided by opposing elements from within. In this type of conflict, disagreeing ideas in the protagonist struggle for the upper hand. The protagonist must make a difficult decision.

An example is a girl who is tempted to cheat on an exam, even though she is basically an honest person. Another example is a man who believes in peace, but must decide whether to fight in self-defense.

Person Versus Nature

Person versus nature means protagonist against the natural elements. In this type of conflict, the protagonist struggles against the forces of nature.

Examples include the sailor whose boat is threatened by a stormy sea, the mountain climber who struggles to get to the top of the mountain, or the camper who fights to stay alive during a surprise snow storm.

Person Versus Fate

Person versus fate means protagonist against destiny or supernatural elements. Many good examples of this type of conflict are found in stories of the ancient Greeks.

In some stories, such as those about Oedipus, the characters struggle to have their way against the will of the gods. Sometimes the character tries to use powers reserved for gods. In other stories, the protagonist tries to outsmart destiny. An example is a character who tries to live forever, even though people are destined to die.

A. Choose the best replacement for the bold words or phrases. Write the letter of your answer on the line.

_____ 1. In many stories, the hero battles the **antagonist.**

_____ 2. Some problems are the result of **things that just happen.**

_____ 3. Surviving a hurricane is an example of person versus **Earth's forces.**

_____ 4. Students in a school are a **group of people with common interests.**

a. society
b. nature
c. fate
d. villain

B. Read the five types of conflict listed below. Identify the type of conflict that each of the following situations represents. Write the correct letter on the line provided.

a. Person versus person
b. Person versus society
c. Person versus self
d. Person versus nature
e. Person versus fate

_____ 1. A bank teller puts a roll of bank money in her purse. She then remembers that her employer trusted her and gave her a job when no one else would hire her.

_____ 2. A dog must fight with the leader of the wolf pack.

_____ 3. A homeless boy cannot find a place to sleep. People of the city keep telling him that trespassing is forbidden and that he must move on.

_____ 4 A man makes a bargain with the devil so that he may be able to read other people's minds.

_____ 5. A robber sets up an ambush in the mountains to stop the sheriff who is chasing him.

_____ 6. Two travelers lose their way in the desert. They must find water soon, or they will die.

_____ 7. A young man cannot get a job in the town in which he lives. People do not like the way he dresses or wears his hair.

_____ 8. A mad scientist creates a living creature in order to have godlike powers over it.

_____ 9. A doctor must decide whether to risk her own life in order to treat a patient with a deadly disease.

_____ 10. Two people cling to a small raft in the ocean. They try to fight their way to shore.

C. Read the paragraph below. Then, identify the three types of conflict that occur in the story.

In the play *Oedipus the King* by the ancient Greek Sophocles, a messenger of the gods tells Oedipus of his destiny. Oedipus does not like what he hears. He decides to defy the gods. He runs away to avoid the events that they have foretold. Because the gods are angry with Oedipus, they send a terrible sickness to the people of the city where Oedipus has become king. An old blind prophet tells Oedipus that the sickness is his fault. Oedipus becomes very angry with the prophet. They argue and call one another names. Eventually, the story of Oedipus becomes known to the people, and they banish him from the city.

1. The flight of Oedipus from his foretold destiny is an example of person versus _____ .

2. The argument between Oedipus and the blind prophet is an example of person

    versus_____ .

3. The banishment of Oedipus by the people is an example of person versus _____ .

D. Read the paragraph below. Then, in your own words, describe an example of each type of conflict that occurs in the story.

In the story "Gulliver the Great" by Walter A. Dyer, a man named Enderby is a passenger on a ship that blows up in the water. Enderby gets away on a raft by himself. He is alone in the ocean with no land in sight. As he floats along, he sees Gulliver, a huge dog from the ship, swimming toward him. Enderby is terrified of dogs. He and Gulliver have not been friends aboard the ship. The man wonders in a panic if Gulliver will attack him. He considers hitting Gulliver over the head with an oar. Instead, in spite of his fear, he allows the dog to come aboard and shares his little amount of food and water with him.

1. Person versus person: _____

    _____

2. Person versus nature: _____

    _____

3. Person versus self: _____

    _____

Lesson 2

Structure

Introduction

Plot is a series of planned, related incidents that happen in a story. However, it does not contain every thought or every action of the characters. The parts of a plot are planned by the author. The order in which the parts are presented is also decided by the author. This planned order of events in a story is called the structure.

Details to Omit

A single character has as many thoughts and actions as a real person. Including all this detail would create books that are huge and boring. For example, in most stories, readers do not care about the details of the character getting out of bed, turning off his alarm clock, deciding what to wear, dressing himself, eating breakfast, or brushing his teeth.

Likewise, situations that have no effect on a story are not needed. For example, in a story about a family of ten living in a one-room house, knowing that the neighbor's mother lives in a red house probably has no bearing on the story. Unneeded facts confuse readers and can make stories move slowly.

The author, therefore, will select only those thoughts and incidents which are important to the story. Of all the possible thoughts, emotions, and incidents that might concern a character, the author uses only a few.

Plot Structure

A plot must have more than one incident, and each incident must be related to the others. This is why a plot is called a series of planned, related incidents.

The author selects some point in the character's life at which to begin the story. This order could be: beginning, middle, end. For example, an author could tell the story of a person's life in the order in which events occurred: birth and early childhood, teenage years, adulthood, middle age, old age, death. A sports story could present a game with minute-by-minute accounts, just as each event occurs. Both stories would use the same order: beginning, middle, and end.

Literature Terms

flashback

exposition

rising action

climax

falling action

denouement

in medias res

A person's life story could begin in the middle with other details following. Likewise, a sportswriter could report on yesterday's game by starting to describe an exciting moment in that game. Then the ending (the score) and the beginning (pre-game activities) could be added. In both types of stories, the events are not told in the order in which they occurred.

Flashback is one main way for an author to tell the ending first and then fill in the beginning. This technique shows the characters thinking or talking about events that happened earlier. For example, an author describes the present life of a famous person. Then details about earlier events, perhaps childhood or education, are added. These earlier events are told in flashback. Again, the description of events is no longer in the order in which those events occurred.

The selection and planned order in which the author arranges these thoughts, emotions, and incidents is called the plot structure. By arranging the plot in a certain structure, the author can choose what to emphasize. The ancient Greeks compared plot to the tying of a knot followed by the untying of a knot. The various conflicts included in the story are the different threads of the knot.

In most stories, a conflict is introduced. This conflict may get very complicated. Other conflicts occur. The reader is kept in suspense for a time. Finally, there is a turning point. The complications begin to be clear to the reader. By the end of the story, the conflicts are usually resolved and explained.

Freytag's Pyramid of Dramatic Structure

The basic plot structure used in most short stories, novels, plays, and narrative poetry has five parts. These five parts can be pictured as a triangle or a pyramid like the one pictured below. A similar pyramid was first used by a 19th-century German writer named Gustav Freytag. Therefore, such a pyramid is called Freytag's Pyramid of Dramatic Structure.

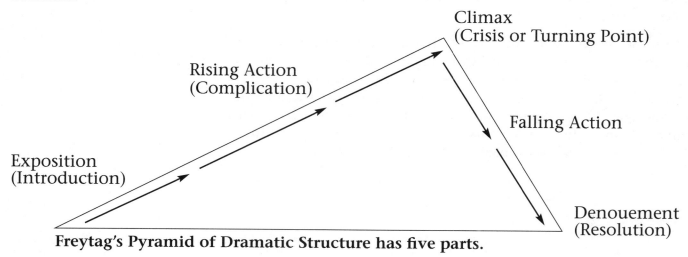

Freytag's Pyramid of Dramatic Structure has five parts.

Explanation of Freytag's Pyramid

The **exposition** is sometimes called the introduction. It usually comes early in a story and gives the reader information that is necessary for understanding the story. For instance, some of the characters are introduced. The setting is at least partly described. Explanations are given for important events that happened before the story begins.

The **rising action** is sometimes called the complication. This section is the longest part of most stories. During the rising action, conflicts are introduced. The conflicts might become complicated. The readers are kept in suspense about what the characters will do and how the conflicts will turn out.

The **climax** is sometimes called the crisis or the turning point. The climax is the point of highest interest in a story. It is the point at which a character takes some action that leads either to disaster or to a happy ending. Because the action taken at the climax determines how the story turns out, the climax is also called the turning point.

The **falling action** follows the climax and begins to explain the complications to the reader. The falling action is usually much shorter than the rising action. By now, the reader has some idea how the story will turn out. Often, however, an author will include a final moment of suspense when it looks as if things might not go the way they seemed to be going.

The **denouement** is the unraveling of the knot. The word denouement means "to untie." At the denouement, all the loose ends of the plot are made clear to the reader. Perhaps the identity of the villain becomes known. Perhaps families are reunited. Perhaps mistaken identities are cleared up. All the secrets and complications of the plot are revealed.

In Medias Res

The five-part structure listed above is the most common plot structure. These five parts usually occur in the order listed. Of course, an author is free to use variations. Authors are free to omit any part of the structure or to change the order.

One very popular variation on the pyramid structure is the story which begins *in medias res.* This Latin phrase means "in the middle of things." Authors might wish to begin, without explanation, at a particularly exciting part of the story. This device gets the reader's interest quickly.

If a story begins *in medias res,* the exposition and some of the rising action will be filled in for the reader by flashbacks.

Plot

A. Choose the best replacement for the bold words or phrases. Write the letter of your answer on the line.

_____ 1. Kaydra's graduation marked the **turning point** in the story.

_____ 2. Kaydra's home problems become clear in the **wind down.**

_____ 3. In the **beginning of the story** Kaydra was in kindergarten.

_____ 4. The **presenting of earlier events** made Kaydra's fears more clear.

_____ 5. During the **final wrap up** Kaydra and a friend get an apartment.

_____ 6. During the **presentation of details** Kaydra struggled with school.

_____ 7. Stories that begin **in the middle of the action** usually grab readers' interest quickly.

a. flashback

b. exposition

c. rising action

d. climax

e. falling action

f. denouement

g. _in medias res_

B. Write the parts of the structure pyramid on the lines provided. Put them in the order in which they usually occur. Be sure to spell them correctly.

1. _____

2. _____

3. _____

4. _____

5. _____

C. The five parts of Freytag's pyramid are shown in the diagram below. Identify the area on the pyramid into which each of the following items would most likely fit. Write the letter of the correct answer on the line.

c. Climax
(Crisis or Turning Point)

b. Rising Action
(Complication)

d. Falling Action

a. Exposition
(Introduction)

e. Denouement
(Resolution)

_____ 1. The protagonist is introduced as an ambitious person.

_____ 2. The protagonist makes a decision which determines that all will end happily.

_____ 3. The antagonist makes life very difficult for the protagonist.

_____ 4. The reader gets a clearer idea of how the story will end.

_____ 5. The setting is described.

_____ 6. The complications are all made clear to the reader.

_____ 7. The protagonist completely changes, indicating that the story will have a surprise ending.

_____ 8. A final moment of suspense occurs.

_____ 9. The conflicts are all resolved.

_____ 10. New problems are introduced.

Unit 6
Theme

Lesson 1

The Main Idea

Introduction

The **theme** of a story is its main idea. Every story is based on a main idea and controlled by that main idea.

Authors observe that when people behave in certain ways, certain things happen to them. They form some ideas about life and about human nature. Authors of fiction communicate these ideas to readers through characters, settings, and plots.

Theme Search

To determine the main idea of a story, it is necessary to look closely at every part of a story. Character, setting, and plot help to get this main idea across. Sometimes images and symbols also reinforce the main idea.

Some useful questions to ask are:

- What sort of people are the characters?

- What are their values and attitudes?

- Where do they go?

- What do they do?

- What do they say?

- What happens to them as a result of what they do and say?

By adding all this information together, readers can determine the theme or main idea of a story.

Sometimes a story will have more than one theme. If there is one idea that is emphasized more than others, it is called the **main theme.** Others are called lesser themes or **minor themes.**

Theme Statements

Single words are not descriptive enough to be a story theme. To say that a story is about "love" does not really express an idea. Is love rewarding? Is love painful? Does love enable people to overcome handicaps? Does love cause people to do foolish things? A theme needs to be a meaningful statement made up of a group of words.

A. Read the information given in each situation below. Then, read the three possible theme statements. Circle the letter of the theme statement which is **not** a likely possibility to express the main idea.

1. While traveling west looking for work, the Joad family's group of twelve people face many hardships. They meet up with the Wilsons, a married couple with a broken down car. Al Joad fixes the Wilson's vehicle. Ma and Pa invite the Wilsons to travel with the family rather than risking the trip alone. The newly enlarged group moves safely on.

    a. People have a natural responsibility and compassion for others.

    b. Helping others is sometimes ill advised.

    c. Human kindness overshadows hardships.

2. A newcomer to the Yukon sets out with his dog on a day when the temperature is 75 degrees below zero. He ignores the advice of people who have been in the North longer than he has. He believes that he is a match for any condition the climate can bring about. He soon realizes that his fingers, toes, and face are frozen. He is far from help, and he is freezing to death.

    a. A determined person can overcome any odds.

    b. Humans must respect the forces of nature if they want to survive.

    c. Pride goes before a fall.

3. Janie grew up to be a modern African American woman searching for equality in her life. She left one husband and was widowed by a second before she found a husband she could relate to as an equal. Upon the tragic death of her third husband, she returns to her home town where she faces the curiosity of the townspeople. Having experienced the comfort of living with equality, Janie is confident enough to ignore gossip.

    a. A feeling of equality can comfort the other senses.

    b. If you can't be equal at home, you can't be equal anywhere.

    c. It's hard to go home after a tragedy.

(continued on the next page)

4. Throughout the years of his career, a locomotive engineer passes the same house daily. He waves to the family that lives in it. They always cheerfully wave back to him. He feels that the members of this family have become his friends. He decides that he will pay them a visit when he retires. He looks forward to this visit for a long time. The day comes when he knocks on the family's door. They do not recognize him and treat him coldly and suspiciously. They also treat each other rudely. In fact, they turn out to be very unpleasant people. The engineer is hurt and disappointed.

   a. Things are not always what they appear to be.

   b. Making judgments without enough knowledge can lead to disappointment.

   c. It is better never to trust anybody.

5. Miss Dove is unmarried and has devoted her entire life to teaching. She cares for her students and thinks about them often. She is not, however, a popular teacher. She has a reputation for being extremely strict. She demands higher standards of work and behavior than do other teachers in her school. As she grows older, Miss Dove begins to wonder if she has ever done anything really worthwhile in her life. Has she made any difference to anybody? One day, she learns that one of her favorite former students, Thomas, has been a prisoner of war. Thomas survived, she learns from his little brother, because he had learned self-discipline as a little boy in Miss Dove's class. Thomas learned to control himself because he had been so afraid of Miss Dove.

   a. People are not always aware at the time of the influence that they have on others.

   b. Teachers should not be so hard on their students.

   c. Sometimes people show caring in unexpected ways.

B. Read each situation and complete the theme statement for each situation.

1. Two teenagers are members of feuding families. They fall in love and want to marry. The feud, however, leads to the death of these teenagers. Instead of a wedding, there is a double funeral. Both families will die out because the two teenagers were the only children.

   Theme statement: Hatred and prejudice _____

   _____

2. A group of young schoolboys are stranded on a south sea island. Their plane has been shot down during a war. The boys decide to build a better civilization than they left behind. All goes well at first. Eventually, however, they are quarreling, fighting, and even killing one another.

   Theme statement: Human nature _____

   _____

(continued on the next page)

3. The greedy King Midas is granted his wish that everything he touches will turn into gold. For a brief time, he enjoys his increasing wealth. However, the king has a daughter who means more to him than anything on earth. One day he turns her pet cat into gold. His daughter, naturally, is upset. Forgetting his new power, the king hugs his daughter. She also turns into gold. In the process, of course, she dies.

   Theme statement: Greed _____

   _____

4. After being framed and wrongfully shunned by his fellow townspeople, Silas Marner decides to live a solitary life and focus only on collecting gold. When his fortune is stolen, he sinks into despair until an orphaned two-year-old enters his life. He discovers the richness of love far surpasses the richness of gold.

   Theme statement: True wealth _____

   _____

5. A young panther nearly loses his life in a fight with a cougar. He gets the worst of several more fights. Finally, he sits down and thinks about what has happened. He realizes that his own carelessness has caused his problems. Later, he wins a fight with another stronger panther.

   Theme statement: Experience _____

   _____

For Further Learning: Read the stories on which the activities for this lesson were based. Some are short stories, some are plays, and others are novels.

Activity B
1. *The Grapes of Wrath* by John Steinbeck
2. "To Build a Fire" by Jack London
3. *Their Eyes Were Watching God* by Zora Neale Hurston
4. "The Far and the Near" by Thomas Wolfe
5. "The *Terrible* Miss Dove" by Frances Gray Patton

Activity C
1. *Romeo and Juliet* by William Shakespeare
2. *Lord of the Flies* by William Golding
3. "King Midas" in any collection of Greek mythology
4. *Silas Marner* by George Eliot
5. "The White Panther" by Theodore J. Waldeck

Unit 7
Style and Technique

Lesson 1

Point of View

Introduction

Style is the way in which an author arranges words to express ideas. It is an individual matter. Authors all have their own styles.

Some authors use long sentences and difficult words. Others prefer short sentences and simple words. Some authors use detailed descriptions. Others prefer action to description. Some authors include a great deal of **dialogue.** Other authors have no conversation between the characters.

Certain elements of an author's style may be the same from writing to writing. For instance, an author might use long sentences and vivid descriptions. Other parts of an author's style will change to suit the ideas of a specific story.

One of the elements that an author can change from story to story is **point of view.** Point of view is the angle from which the author presents the actions of the story. The author determines the point of view by choosing a **narrator.** Narrator means a person who tells a story. Authors select a certain point of view depending upon what they wish to emphasize.

First person and third person are the two basic points of view. Authors use different variations of these two versions. The three most common variations of points of view are:

- First person narrator
- Third person narrator/limited
- Third person narrator/omniscient

Literature Terms

style

dialogue

point of view

narrator

limited

omniscient

First Person Narrator

The first person narrator will use first person pronouns when referring to himself or herself. A pronoun is a word that is used to take the place of a noun. The first person pronouns are *I, my, me, mine, we, us, our,* and *ours.* If a narrator uses these pronouns to refer to himself or herself, the story is told in first person point of view.

The first person narrator is a character in the story who is telling the story in his or her own words. For example, if Karen is the narrator, she can tell only those things that she can know by observation. Karen can see what is happening only in scenes in which she is present. She can know what other characters tell her. She can comment upon what she thinks. Karen cannot, however, see into the minds of other characters and report their thoughts.

The first person narrator is usually the main character, but this is not always the case. A minor character or an observer who has no part in the action may also narrate the story.

An example of a story with a first person narrator is "Six Feet of the Country" by Nadine Gordimer. The narrator is a Johannesburg man. He is also a main character in this story about South Africa. Read the selection from this story given below. Notice the pronoun *I* that is used to tell the story.

> The little boy who had been left to watch the donkeys dropped the reins and ran to see. I don't know why—unless it was for the same reason people crowd round someone who has fainted in a cinema—but I parted the wires of the fence and went through after him.

Third Person Narrator/Limited

The third person narrator will use the pronouns *he, she, it, they, his, hers, its, theirs, him, her,* or *them.* If the narrator uses these pronouns even when referring to himself or herself, the story is told from the third person point of view. The third person narrator will not be a character in the story.

The third person **limited** point of view is a variation of this technique. Here the author may choose to limit the point of view to the viewpoint of one character. Only events which concern this one character are presented.

An example of the third person limited point of view can be found in the story "The Member of the Wedding" by Carson McCullers. The entire story is told from the point of view of the main character, Frankie. Frankie, however, does not tell the story herself.

The story begins with Frankie, a twelve-year-old girl, feeling uncertain of her place in the world. She spends some lazy summer days with six-year-old John Henry who is not yet searching for answers. Notice the pronouns *she, her, he, him,* and *herself* that are used to tell Frankie's story.

> She stood on the sidewalk, looking at John Henry, and the smart political remark came back to her. She hooked her thumb in the pockets of her pants and asked: "If you were going to vote in an election, who would you vote for?"
>
> John Henry's voice was bright and high in the summer night. "I don't know," he said.
>
> "For instance, would you cast your vote for C.P. MacDonald to be mayor of this town?"
>
> John Henry did not answer.
>
> "Would you?" But she could not get him to talk. There were times when John Henry would not answer anything you said to him. So she had to remark without an argument behind her, and all by herself like that it did not sound so very smart: "Why, I wouldn't vote for him if he was running to be dog-catcher."

Third Person Narrator/Omniscient

The third person **omniscient** point of view is another possibility. The word omniscient means "all-knowing." The author may choose for the narrator to know everything about all characters. If the narrator knows all things, including what goes on in the character's thoughts, the narrator is called a third person omniscient narrator.

An example of the third person omniscient point of view is the story *Animal Farm* by George Orwell. The narrator of this story knows the actions and thoughts of all the characters. The unspoken thoughts and feelings of the animals are revealed to the reader.

In the scene on the next page, the animals experience their first chance to work for themselves. Although none of them narrates the story, the omniscient narrator knows all their thoughts and feelings.

All through that summer the work of the farm went like clockwork. The animals were happy as they had never conceived it possible to be. Every mouthful of food was an acute positive pleasure, now that it was truly their own food, produced by themselves and for themselves, not doled out to them by a grudging master. . . .They met with many difficulties, . . . but the pigs with their cleverness and Boxer with his tremendous muscles always pulled them through. Boxer was the admiration of everybody. . . . His answer to every problem, every setback, was "I will work harder!"— which he had adopted as his personal motto.

But everybody worked according to his capacity. . . . Nobody stole, nobody grumbled over his rations, the quarreling and biting and jealousy which had been normal features of life in the old days had almost disappeared.

A. Choose the best replacement for the bold words or phrases. Write the letter of your answer on the line.

_____ 1. The story included no **conversation between characters.**

_____ 2. The two authors' **ways of arranging words** were very different.

_____ 3. The main character was also the **person telling the story.**

_____ 4. The **angle from which the story is told** kept much information from the readers.

_____ 5. The narrator had an **all-knowing** knowledge of the story.

_____ 6. The story was written in **a way that uses** *I, we, us,* **and** *me.*

_____ 7. The narrator had a **less than complete** knowledge of other characters.

_____ 8. The story was written in **a way that uses** *he, she,* **and** *they.*

a. styles

b. dialogue

c. point of view

d. narrator

e. first person

f. third person

g. limited

h. omniscient

B. Show your understanding of point of view. Choose the word from the box that correctly completes each of the following sentences. Write that word on the line provided.

omniscient	thoughts	third
character	first	observation
main	pronouns	limited
not		

1. The first person narrator is a _____ in the story who tells what happens in his or her own words.

2. The first person narrator can tell only those things learned by _____ or by what other characters say.

3. The first person narrator cannot see into the minds of other characters to know their _____ .

4. The first person narrator will usually be the _____ character.

5. The third person narrator is _____ a character in the story.

6. The story has a third person _____ point of view when the third person narrator tells the story from the viewpoint of only one character.

7. The story has a third person _____ point of view when the narrator knows everything about all of the characters.

8. One basic point of view is _____ person. It uses pronouns such as *I* and *me.*

9. One basic point of view is _____ person. It uses pronouns such as *he, she* and *they.*

10. By looking at the _____ that the narrator uses, you can easily tell the difference between the two basic points of view.

C. Read the five sentences below. Identify the point of view in each passage. Write the correct letter on the line provided.

a. first person point of view   **b.** third person point of view

_____ 1. "I didn't want to fool with Hade. For every time he'd ever stopped me in his life, he wanted to borrow something from me or he wanted me to do something for him."

_____ 2. "Miss Dove was waiting for the sixth grade to file in for its geography lesson. She stood behind her desk, straight as the long map pointer in her hand. And suddenly she had the feeling of not being really alone."

_____ 3. "An abrupt sound startled him. Off to the right he heard it; and his ears, expert in such matters, could not be mistaken. Again, he heard the sound, and again."

_____ 4. "I now summoned the boys to assist me in procuring blocks of wood for my crushing machine, and the following day we set forth with saws, ropes, axes, and other tools. We soon reached the tree I had selected for my purpose, and I began by sending Fritz and Jack up into the tree with axes to cut off the larger of the high branches so that, when the tree fell, it would not injure its neighbors."

_____ 5. "When he looked up again, it was dark outside and he saw the bright rim of the moon just peeping over the horizon. He jumped up in a great fright and rang for the Court Jester. The Court Jester came bounding into the room and sat down at the foot of the throne."

For Further Learning: Read the stories from which the examples in Activity C are taken.

1. "Fight Number Twenty-five" by Jesse Stuart
2. "The *Terrible* Miss Dove" by Frances Gray Patton
3. "The Most Dangerous Game" by Richard Connell
4. *The Swiss Family Robinson* by Johann David Wyss
5. *Many Moons* by James Thurber

Lesson 2

Imagery

Introduction

Imagery is the combination of words or phrases to create pictures in the reader's mind. Like point of view, it is part of an author's style.

Most imagery in stories is visual. It is intended to make the reader see something or someone clearly. Imagery can also appeal to touch, taste, smell, and sound.

Imagery is a form of the word *image,* which means picture. Any time an author uses words to create the idea of a sight, touch, taste, smell, or sound in readers' minds, the author is using imagery.

Words and phrases that are most often used to create images are adjectives, verbs, and comparisons.

Adjectives

Adjectives are words that describe. Adjectives can tell which one, what kind, or how many. They most often appear immediately before the noun they describe, for example: The <u>tall green</u> (weeds) were near the river. Other times, adjectives are placed just after a verb, for example: The weeds near the river (were) <u>tall</u> and <u>green</u>.

The more precise and colorful the adjectives are, the more exact and realistic images they create.

Verbs

Verbs are the action words of a sentence as shown in this example: The fish <u>jumped</u> out of the water. Jumped is an action that can be physically demonstrated.

Verbs can also express a state of being. For example, in the following sentence, the verb does not tell what the fish is doing. The verb is simply states that the fish exists: The fish <u>is</u> in the water.

Sometimes verbs can serve as helpers for other verbs. Study this example: The fish was lying on the grass. In this example, the verb *lying* explains the action in the sentence. A second verb *was* is used as a helping word for *lying.*

When stories have vivid verbs, the stories are more exciting for readers. Active verbs let readers create a detailed image of the action.

Literature Terms

imagery

simile

metaphor

Comparisons

A comparison points out the way in which two things are alike. The two most useful kinds of phrases to show comparison are similes and metaphors. A **simile** is a comparison which uses like or as. Study these examples:

The fog was like a heavy gray blanket.

Amber is like a scared rabbit.

A **metaphor** is a comparison which does not use like or as. A metaphor directly states that one item is the same as another. Study these examples:

The fog was a heavy gray blanket.

Amber is a scared rabbit.

Fresh and original comparisons make stories more interesting to readers. Vivid comparisons help readers see what the author sees.

A. Choose the best replacement for the bold words or phrases. Write the letter of your answer on the line.

_____ 1. The phrase *like a simile* can help people remember the name of a **comparison that uses *like* or *as.***

_____ 2. The **combination of words and phrases used to create pictures** was colorful and vivid.

_____ 3. The most direct type of comparison is a **comparison that does not use *like* or *as.***

    a. imagery

    b. simile

    c. metaphor

B. Read the sentences below. Replace each of the adjectives in parentheses with a more precise or colorful adjective.

1. She was a _____ (nice) lady.

2. He was a _____ (large) man.

3. The dog had a _____ (mean) temper.

4. Her eyes were a _____ (pretty) shade of blue.

5. Joan had a _____ (big) talent for singing.

6. Monday had been a _____ (bad) day for Jim.

7. This is a _____ (good) chocolate cake.

8. The smell of the garbage was _____ (unpleasant).

C. The passages below are from "The White Panther" by Theodore J. Waldeck. The story is about a white jungle cat named Ku-Ma. Circle the adjectives used in the passages below. Then, create summaries by writing the adjectives in the blanks.

1. "To Ku-Ma, life was still a mysterious and baffling thing."

   Life is _____ and _____ .

2. "He was learning . . . the hard way, the only way savage creatures can learn the lore of the jungle—by bitter, hand-to-hand experience."

   a. How many ways to learn? _____ .

   b. The creatures are _____ .

   c. The experience is _____ and _____ .

3. "First one monkey would suck in air, distend his drumlike throat, and let loose with his shuddering roar."

   a. How many monkeys? _____ .

   b. The monkey's throat is _____ .

   c. The monkey's roar is _____ .

4. "Throwing caution to the winds, Ku-Ma emitted a snarl of baffled rage and plunged through the dense thicket ahead."

   a. The rage is _____ .

   b. The thicket is _____ .

5. "In an instant the sunlit glade crashed and echoed with the spitting, snarling fury of two great cats in deadly combat."

   a. The glade is _____ .

   b. The cats' fury is _____ and _____ .

   c. How many cats? _____

   d. The cats are _____ .

   e. Their combat is _____ .

6. "He did not know that his opponent was older and wiser than he . . ."

   The opponent is _____ and _____ .

D. The story "The White Panther" is full of vivid action verbs. Circle the verb, or action word, in each passage below.

1. "Ku-Ma's jaws dripped in anticipation."

2. "Overhead a group of ringtail monkeys ceased their acrobatics . . ."

3. "Ku-Ma emitted a snarl of baffled rage."

4. "Furious, seething, he bared his teeth . . ."

5. "Blindly he rolled free . . ."

6. "Then abruptly Ku-Ma stiffened."

7. "For a long moment the two great cats eyed each other. . . ."

8. "Ku-Ma . . . limped painfully to a moss-covered spot."

E. It is possible to improve the image or change the meaning by changing the verb. Write two vivid synonyms of the verb *said* in each of the sentences below. The first sentence has been done as an example.

1. "Don't come near me," he said.

   "Don't come near me," he <u>pleaded</u>.

   "Don't come near me," he <u>hissed</u>.

2. "Stop!," she said.

   "Stop!" she _____ .

   "Stop!" she _____ .

3. "I'm leaving," he said.

   "I'm leaving," he _____ .

   "I'm leaving," he _____ .

4. "No," she said.

   "No," she _____ .

   "No," she _____ .

5. "I heard you," he said.

   "I heard you," he _____ .

   "I heard you," he _____ .

F.   Read the comparisons. If the comparison is a simile, write *S*. If it is a metaphor, write *M*.

_____   1.   The snow was a blanket of white.

_____   2.   Stars twinkled like Christmas tree lights.

_____   3.   The night was as still as death.

_____   4.   She was the apple of his eye.

_____   5.   The cold was like a knife.

_____   6.   The wind was a knife of cold air.

_____   7.   The sight of home was heaven to him.

_____   8.   The long river looked like a snake slithering between high rocks.

_____   9.   The dog's shrill barks were like the firing of a machine gun.

_____ 10.   The sudden thought was a thunderbolt in his brain.

G.   Complete the comparisons below to create imagery of your own.

1.   Her eyes were as blue as _____ .

2.   The sunset exploded like _____ .

3.   In the distance the tall pine trees looked like _____ .

4.   The wind was moaning like _____ .

5.   He felt as strong as _____ .

6.   Her laughter sounded like _____ .

7.   The rain falling on the tin roof sounded like _____ .

8.   The silken scarf was as soft as _____ .

9.   Surprisingly, the medicine tasted as good as _____ .

10.   The rain falling on the tin roof sounded like _____ .

Mastery Lesson #3

A. Read or review the story "The Lady, or the Tiger?" by Frank Stockton. You will find it in Appendix A beginning on page 84.

B. Several different types of conflict are used in this story. Identify each item below according to the type of conflict it represents. One type is not used. Write the correct letters on the lines provided. If necessary, review pages 53–54.

a. person versus person   d. person versus nature

b. person versus society   e. person versus fate

c. person versus self

_____ 1. The young man breaks a law of the kingdom by loving the princess.

_____ 2. The princess hates the young woman behind the door.

_____ 3. The outcome of the trials usually depended upon chance.

_____ 4. The princess has to make a terrible decision about whether or not she will help the young man to live.

C. Read the theme statements below. Decide if each could be a possible theme for this story. Put an X in front of those theme statements which are possibilities. If necessary, review pages 62–63.

_____ 1. True love may involve sacrifices

_____ 2. It is difficult to give up a loved one to someone else.

_____ 3. Barbaric attitudes lead to fair trials.

_____ 4. It may become very important for people in love to understand each other very well.

_____ 5. It does not really matter whom one marries.

_____ 6. Barbaric forms of justice can be very cruel.

_____ 7. True love causes a person to consider the welfare of the loved one.

_____ 8. Common people should know better than to love princesses.

D. Read the events from the story below. Place the letter of each event on the appropriate line on the pyramid. Some lines will requre more than one letter. Some lines may not be used at all. If necessary, review pages 58–59.

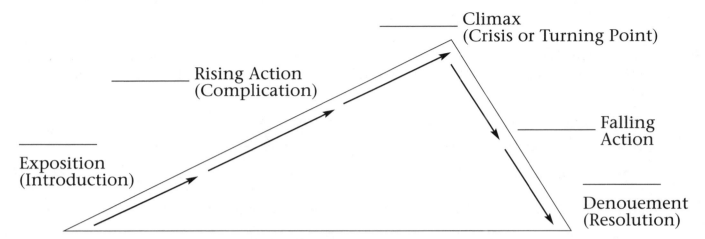

a. The king is introduced and described.

b. The young man realizes that the princess knows which door is in front of the tiger.

c. The young man is arrested.

d. The time is identified as "in the very olden time."

e. The method of the trial is described.

f. The day of the trial arrives.

g. The thoughts of the princess are revealed.

h. The arena is described.

i. The young man opens a door.

j. The princess moves her hand towards the right.

k. The princess is introduced and described.

l. The attitude of the princess toward the lady is revealed.

E. Look at the completed pyramid above. This story is somewhat unusual because two parts of the pyramid are not used at all. Complete the sentences below. Write your answers on the lines provided.

1. The longest part of this story fits into the _____ part of the pyramid.

2. The _____ and the _____ are the two parts that the reader must supply. Because this story ends in a way that the reader would not expect, it is said to have a surprise ending.

F. Circle the answer that correctly completes each sentence.

1. This story does not include any _____ .

   a. rising action   **b.** dialogue   **c.** protagonist

2. This story is told from the _____ point of view.

   a. first person   **b.** young man's   **c.** third person limited

3. A narrator who is _____ knows all things.

   a. put in prison   **b.** brilliant   **c.** omniscient

4. The _____ can see into the thoughts of the characters.

   a. narrator   **b.** princess   **c.** king

5. Since this story is not in first person, there is no _____ .

   a. conclusion   **b.** mystery   **c.** use of the pronoun "I"

6. "The Lady, or the Tiger?" does not make use of _____ .

   a. description   **b.** *in medias res*   **c.** climax

7. It is a _____ when the author calls the onlookers in the arena a vast ocean of anxious faces.

   a. simile   **b.** metaphor   **c.** mistake

G. On your own paper, write an ending for this story in two or three paragraphs. As you write, keep these things in mind:

- Begin at the point where the young man opens the door.
- Try to choose good descriptive adjectives.
- Use vivid verbs.
- Include one or two fitting comparisons.
- Be sure to tell what happens to the young man and to the princess.
- After you have finished, check your spelling and punctuation.

End-of-Book Test

A. Read each sentence. If the sentence is true, write *True.* If it is false, write *False.*

_____ 1. During the rising action, all the readers' questions are answered.

_____ 2. Readers can sense a character's personality through other characters' comments.

_____ 3. "On June 27, 1955, at 11:30 A.M." is a specific time setting.

_____ 4. In third person omniscient, the narrator knows the thoughts of all the characters.

_____ 5. Single words make good story themes.

_____ 6. Some fiction is true and some is not true.

_____ 7. Vivid verbs make stories more lively and exciting.

_____ 8. Static characters change a lot during a story.

_____ 9. All authors have their own styles.

_____ 10. Name titles are chosen to stress a main character.

B. Match each item on the left with the correct detail on the right. Write your answer on the line.

_____ 1. fiction genres

_____ 2. climax

_____ 3. philosophy

_____ 4. setting

_____ 5. antagonist

_____ 6. adjectives

_____ 7. theme

_____ 8. narrative

_____ 9. novel

_____ 10. denouement

a. long, purple, heavy, jagged

b. time and place

c. book-length story

d. the turning point in a story

e. short story, novel, play, narrative poem

f. main idea of a story

g. is at odds with the hero of the story

h. basic ideas about life

i. conclusion or resolution of a story

j. words that tell a story

C. Circle the word or phrase in parentheses that correctly completes each sentence.

1. When the pronoun (I, they, you) is often used, the story is in first person.

2. Readers get underlying messages by (reading between the lines, peeking at the ending, asking).

3. A good character must be (a hero, believable, honest).

4. A symbol that is understood by everyone is (boring, universal, useless).

5. Dynamic characters must change (internally, externally, both internally and externally).

6. Princess Daisy is a (place, name, plot, idea) title.

7. The geographical location of a story is (specific or general, not needed, rarely given).

8. Most writing is done in (stanzas, verses, prose).

9. Characters' beliefs, values, and attitudes make up their (external, internal, overactive) selves.

10. The sentence "He moves like a grasshopper." includes a (metaphor, simile, villain).

11. A (dialogue, climax, poem) uses verses or stanzas.

12. Writing that is based on facts is called (fiction, nonfiction, omniscient).

13. A(n) (adjective, verb, prose) is a word that describes.

14. The (denouement, falling action, rising action) presents the details of a story.

15. A character that changes by the end of a story is (static, lyric, dynamic).

D. Choose the answer that correctly completes each sentence. Write the letter of the correct answer on the line.

1. In old Greek stories, the classical hero was always male, courageous, and of _____ .

    a. great humor   **b.** Italian descent   **c.** weak character   **d.** noble birth

2. One of the purposes of the setting is to make the story more _____ .

    a. confusing   **b.** realistic   **c.** like television   **d.** poetic

3. The sentence "He is a rock." includes a _____ .

    a. lyric   **b.** simile   **c.** fact   **d.** metaphor

4. Literature gives us a chance to live through our _____ .

    a. ancestors   **b.** libraries   **c.** teachers   **d.** imaginations

5. A main character that can be either male or female is called the _____

    a. antagonist   **b.** protagonist   **c.** hero   **d.** heroine

6. Clues about the time a story takes place might include historical events, actual people, methods of transportation, and _____ .

    a. styles of dress   **b.** a clock   **c.** a summary   **d.** rising action

7. A _____ is a written sketch that can be used to create a mental picture.

    a. novel   **b.** photograph   **c.** description   **d.** conclusion

8. A heroine successfully reinvents herself following a terrible accident. The conflict in this story is an example of _____ .

    a. person vs. person   **b.** person vs. nature   **c.** person vs. self   **d.** person vs. fate

9. The short story and the play are two different fiction _____ .

    a. genres   **b.** mistakes   **c.** novels   **d.** characters

10. Likes and dislikes, feelings, habits, ambitions, concerns and _____ all contribute to a character's personality.

    a. money   **b.** relatives   **c.** nice skin   **d.** actions

E. Answer the following questions with complete sentences.

1. Explain the difference between the realistic level and the symbolic level of a story.

   _____

   _____

   _____

   _____

2. Explain the difference between a flat character and a round character.

   _____

   _____

   _____

   _____

3. What is the difference between literature and popular fiction?

   _____

   _____

   _____

   _____

4. Explain why a plot must always include a struggle or conflict of some kind.

   _____

   _____

   _____

   _____

5. Literature lets readers experience the emotions and ideas of others. Of what value is this experience?

   _____

   _____

   _____

   _____

Appendix A

The Lady, or the Tiger?
by Frank Stockton

In the very olden time, there lived a **semi-barbaric** king, whose ideas, though somewhat polished and sharpened by the **progressiveness** of distant Latin neighbors, were still large, **florid**, and **untrammeled**, as became the half of him which was barbaric. He was a man of exuberant fancy, and, **withal**, of an authority so irresistible that, at his will, he turned his varied fancies into facts. He was greatly given to **self-communing**; and, when he and himself agreed upon any thing, the thing was done. When every member of his domestic and political systems moved smoothly in its appointed course, his nature was **bland** and **genial**; but whenever there was a little hitch, and some of his orbs got out of their orbits, he was blander and more genial still, for nothing pleased him so much as to make the crooked straight, and crush down uneven places.

Among the borrowed notions by which his barbarism had become **semified** was that of the public arena, in which, by exhibitions of manly and beastly valor, the minds of his subjects were refined and cultured.

But even here the **exuberant** and **barbaric** fancy **asserted** itself. The arena of the king was built, not to give the people an opportunity of hearing the **rhapsodies** of dying gladiators, nor to enable them to view the **inevitable** conclusion of a conflict between religious opinions and hungry jaws, but for purposes far better adapted to widen and develop the mental energies of the people. This vast **amphitheatre**, with its encircling galleries, its mysterious vaults, and its unseen passages, was an agent of poetic justice, in which crime was punished, or virtue rewarded, by the **decrees** of an **impartial** and **incorruptible** chance.

Vocabulary Help

semi-barbaric—half civilized and half barbaric

progressiveness—the state of being advanced or accepting of new ideas

florid—healthy

untrammeled—not bound, free

withal—in addition

self-communing—thinking deeply about oneself

bland—dull, unexciting

genial—friendly

semified—toned down

exuberant—high spirited

barbaric—uncivilized, savage

asserted—put oneself or one's ideas forward

rhapsodies—joyful songs

inevitable—impossible to avoid

amphitheatre—large public arena

decrees—judgments; orders

impartial—fair

incorruptible—honorable

When a subject was accused of a crime of sufficient importance to interest the king, public notice was given that on an appointed day the fate of the accused person would be decided in the king's arena—a structure which well deserved its name; for, although its form and plan were borrowed from afar, its purpose **emanated** solely from the brain of this man, who, every barleycorn a king, knew no tradition to which he owed more allegiance than pleased his fancy, and who ingrafted on every adopted form of human thought and action the rich growth of his barbaric **idealism.**

When all the people had assembled in the galleries, and the king, surrounded by his court, sat high up on his throne of royal state on one side of the arena, he gave a signal, a door beneath him opened, and the accused subject stepped out into the amphitheatre. Directly opposite him, on the other side of the enclosed space, were two doors, exactly alike and side by side. It was the duty and the privilege of the person on trial to walk directly to these doors and open one of them. He could open either door he pleased: he was subject to no **guidance** or influence but that of the aforementioned and impartial and incorruptible chance. If he opened the one, there came out of it a hungry tiger, the fiercest and most cruel that could be **procured,** which immediately sprang upon him, and tore him to pieces, as a punishment for his guilt. The moment that the case of the criminal was thus decided, **doleful** iron bells were clanged, great wails went up from the hired mourners posted on the outer rim of the arena, and the vast audience, with bowed heads and downcast hearts, **wended** slowly their homeward way, mourning greatly that one so young and fair, or so old and respected, should have **merited** so **dire** a fate.

But if the accused person opened the other door, there came forth from it a lady, the most suitable to his years and station that his majesty could select among his fair subjects; and to this lady he was immediately married, as a reward of his innocence. It mattered not that he might already possess a wife and family, or that his affections might be engaged upon an object of his own selection. The king allowed no such **subordinate** arrangements to interfere with his great scheme of **retribution** and reward. The exercises, as in the other instance, took place immediately, and in the arena. Another door opened beneath the king, and a priest, followed by a band of choristers, and dancing maidens blowing joyous airs on golden horns and treading an **epithalamic** measure, advanced to where the pair stood, side by side; and the wedding was promptly and cheerily solemnized. Then the gay brass bells rang forth their merry peals, the people shouted glad hurrahs, and the innocent man, **preceded** by children **strewing** flowers on his path, led his bride to his home.

Vocabulary Help

emanated—came forth

idealism—a belief in the highest standards

guidance—direction, instruction

procured—got or obtained

doleful—sad, mournful

wended—made one's way

merited—deserved

dire—severe; terrible

subordinate—lower; lying beneath

retribution—revenge; a punishment for crime

epithalamic—like a song or poem in honor of a bride and bridegroom

preceded—came before

strewing—scattering widely

This was the king's semi-barbaric method of **administering** justice. Its perfect fairness is obvious. The criminal could not know out of which door would come the lady: he opened either he pleased, without having the slightest idea whether, in the next instant, he was to be devoured or married. On some occasions the tiger came out of one door, and on some out of the other. The decisions of this **tribunal** were not only fair. They were positively determinate: the accused person was instantly punished if he found himself guilty; and, if innocent, he was rewarded on the spot, whether he liked it or not. There was no escape from the judgments of the king's arena.

The **institution** was a very popular one. When the people gathered together on one of the great trial days, they never knew whether they were to witness a bloody slaughter or a **hilarious** wedding. This element of uncertainty lent an interest to the occasion which it could not otherwise have attained. Thus, the masses were entertained and pleased, and the thinking part of the community could bring no charge of unfairness against this plan; for did not the accused person have the whole matter in his own hands?

This semi-barbaric king had a daughter as blooming as his most florid fancies, and with a soul as **fervent** and **imperious** as his own. As is usual in such cases, she was the apple of his eye, and was loved by him above all humanity. Among his courtiers was a young man of that fineness of blood and lowness of station common to the conventional heroes of romance who love royal maidens. This royal maiden was well satisfied with her lover, for he was handsome and brave to a degree **unsurpassed** in all this kingdom; and she loved him with an **ardor** that had enough of barbarism in it to make it exceedingly warm and strong. This love affair moved on happily for many months, until one day the king happened to discover its existence. He did not hesitate nor waver in regard to his duty in the premises. The youth was immediately cast into prison, and a day was appointed for his trial in the king's arena. This, of course, was an especially important occasion; and his majesty, as well as all the people, was greatly interested in the working and development of this trial. Never before had such a case occurred; never before had a subject dared to love the daughter of a king. In after-years such things became commonplace enough; but then they were, in no slight degree, novel and startling.

Vocabulary Help

administering—managing, directing

tribunal—a court of justice

institution—an important custom

hilarious—very funny; high-spirited

fervent—having strong feelings

imperious—bossy, acting like royalty

unsurpassed—best; highest

ardor—deep feeling

The tiger-cages of the kingdom were searched for the most savage and **relentless** beasts, from which the fiercest monster might be selected for the arena; and the ranks of maiden youth and beauty throughout the land were carefully surveyed by **competent** judges, in order that the young man might have a fitting bride in case fate did not determine for him a different destiny. Of course, everybody knew that the deed with which the accused was charged had been done. He had loved the princess, and neither he, she, nor anyone else thought of denying the fact; but the king would not think of allowing any fact of this kind to interfere with the workings of the tribunal, in which he took such great delight and satisfaction. No matter how the affair turned out, the youth would be disposed of; and the king would take an **aesthetic** pleasure in watching the course of events, which would determine whether or not the young man had done wrong in allowing himself to love the princess.

The appointed day arrived. From far and near the people gathered and thronged the great galleries of the arena; and crowds, unable to gain **admittance**, massed themselves against its outside walls. The king and his court were in their places, opposite the twin doors— those fateful **portals**, so terrible in their similarity.

All was ready. The signal was given. A door beneath the royal party opened, and the lover of the princess walked into the arena. Tall, beautiful, fair, his appearance was greeted with a low hum of admiration and anxiety. Half the audience had not known so grand a youth lived among them. No wonder the princess loved him! What a terrible thing for him to be there!

As the youth advanced into the arena, he turned, as the custom was, to bow to the king: but he did not think at all of that royal personage; his eyes were fixed upon the princess, who sat to the right of her father. Had it not been for the **moiety** of barbarism in her nature, it is **probable** that lady would not have been there; but her intense and **fervid** soul would not allow her to be absent on an occasion in which she was so terribly interested. From the moment that the decree had gone forth that her lover should decide his fate in the king's arena, she had thought of nothing, night or day, but this great event and the various subjects connected with it. Possessed of more power, influence, and force of character than any one who had ever before been interested in such a case, she had done what no other person had done,—she had possessed herself of the secret of the doors. She knew in which of the two rooms, that lay behind those doors, stood the cage of the tiger, with its open front, and in which waited the lady. Through these thick doors, heavily curtained with skins on the inside, it was impossible that any noise or suggestion should come from within to the person who should approach to raise the latch of one of them; but gold, and the power of a woman's will, had brought the secret to the princess.

Vocabulary Help

relentless—without pity

competent—able to do something

aesthetic—artistic

admittance—entrance

portals—gates

moiety—half

probable—likely

fervid—burning; passionate

And not only did she know in which room stood the lady ready to emerge, all blushing and **radiant**, should her door be opened, but she knew who the lady was. It was one of the fairest and loveliest of the damsels of the court who had been selected as the reward of the accused youth, should he be proved innocent of the crime of **aspiring** to one so far above him; and the princess hated her. Often had she seen, or imagined that she had seen, this fair creature throwing glances of admiration upon the person of her lover, and sometimes she thought these glances were **perceived** and even returned. Now and then she had seen them talking together; it was but for a moment or two, but much can be said in a brief space; it may have been on most unimportant topics, but how could she know that? The girl was lovely, but she had dared to raise her eyes to the loved one of the princess; and, with all the **intensity** of the savage blood **transmitted** through long lines of wholly barbaric ancestors, she hated the woman who blushed and trembled behind that silent door.

When her lover turned and looked at her, and his eye met hers as she sat there paler and whiter than any one in the vast ocean of anxious faces about her, he saw, by that power of quick **perception** which is given to those whose souls are one, that she knew behind which door crouched the tiger, and behind which stood the lady. He had expected her to know it. He understood her nature, and his soul was assured that she would never rest until she had made plain to herself this thing, hidden to all other lookers-on, even to the king. The only hope for the youth in which there was any element of certainty was based upon the success of the princess in discovering this mystery; and the moment he looked upon her, he saw she had succeeded, as in his soul he knew she would succeed.

Then it was that his quick and anxious glance asked the question: "Which?" It was as plain to her as if he shouted it from where he stood. There was not an instant to be lost. The question was asked in a flash; it must be answered in another.

Her right arm lay on the cushioned **parapet** before her. She raised her hand, and made a slight, quick movement toward the right. No one but her lover saw her. Every eye but his was fixed on the man in the arena.

He turned, and with a firm and rapid step he walked across the empty space. Every heart stopped beating, every breath was held, every eye was fixed immovably upon that man. Without the slightest hesitation, he went to the door on the right, and opened it.

Now the point of the story is this: Did the tiger come out of that door, or did the lady?

Vocabulary Help

radiant—glowing

aspiring—hoping

perceived—understood

intensity—strength

transmitted—sent

perception—understanding

parapet—low wall or railing

Vocabulary Help

The more we reflect upon this question, the harder it is to answer. It involves a study of the human heart which leads us through **devious mazes** of **passion**, out of which it is difficult to find our way. Think of it, fair reader, not as if the decision of the question depended upon yourself, but upon that hot-blooded, semi-barbaric princess, her soul at a white heat beneath the combined fires of despair and jealousy. She had lost him, but who should have him?

How often, in her waking hours and in her dreams, had she started in wild horror, and covered her face with her hands, as she thought of her lover opening the door on the other side of which waited the cruel fangs of the tiger!

But how much oftener had she seen him at the other door! How in her grievous **reveries** had she gnashed her teeth, and torn her hair, when she saw his start of **rapturous** delight as he opened the door of the lady! How her soul had burned in **agony** when she had seen him rush to meet that woman, with her flushing cheek and sparkling eye of triumph; when she had seen him lead her forth, his whole frame kindled with the joy of recovered life; when she had heard the glad shouts from the **multitude**, and the wild ringing of the happy bells; when she had seen the priest, with his joyous followers, advance to the couple, and make them man and wife before her very eyes; and when she had seen them walk away together upon their path of flowers, followed by the tremendous shouts of the hilarious multitude, in which her one despairing shriek was lost and drowned!

Would it not be better for him to die at once, and go to wait for her in the blessed regions of semi-barbaric **futurity?**

And yet, that awful tiger, those shrieks, that blood!

Her decision had been indicated in an instant, but it had been made after days and nights of **anguished deliberation.** She had known she would be asked, she had decided what she would answer, and, without the slightest hesitation, she had moved her hand to the right.

The question of her decision is one not to be lightly considered, and it is not for me to presume to set myself up as the one person able to answer it. And so I leave it with all of you: Which came out of the opened door,—the lady, or the tiger?

devious—crooked; sly

mazes—webs; puzzles

passion—a strong feeling

reveries—daydreams; to be lost in thought

rapturous—extremely happy

agony—great pain

multitude—crowd

futurity—future

anguished—distressed; tormented

deliberation—careful thought

Appendix B

For Further Reading

The following works are referred to in this book. Increase your knowledge of literature by getting the complete versions from your library and reading them.

Aesop. *Aesop's Fables*
Brontë, Charlotte. *Jane Eyre*
Connell, Richard. "The Most Dangerous Game"
Dickens, Charles. *A Tale of Two Cities*
Dickens, Charles. *Oliver Twist*
Doyle, Arthur Conan. "The Adventure of the Speckled Band"
Dyer, Walter A. "Gulliver the Great"
Eliot, George. *Silas Marner*
Golding, William. *Lord of the Flies*
Gordimer, Nadine. "Six Feet of the Country."
Hurston, Zora Neale. *Their Eyes Were Watching God*
Irving, Washington. *The Legend of Sleepy Hollow*
Jacobs, W. W. "The Monkey's Paw"
"King Midas" Any collection of Greek mythology
London, Jack. "To Build a Fire"
McCullers, Carson. *The Member of the Wedding*
Mitchell, Margaret. *Gone With the Wind*
Orwell, George. *Animal Farm*
Patton, Frances Gray. "The *Terrible* Miss Dove"
Shakespeare, William. *Macbeth*
Shakespeare, William. *Romeo and Juliet*
Sophocles. *Oedipus the King*, also called *Oedipus Rex*
Steinbeck, John. *The Grapes of Wrath*
Stockton, Frank. "The Lady, or the Tiger?"
Stuart, Jesse. "Fight Number Twenty-five"
Thurber, James. *Many Moons*
Waldeck, Theodore J. "The White Panther"
Wolfe, Thomas. "The Far and the Near"
Wordsworth, William. "The Daffodils"
Wyss, Johann David. *The Swiss Family Robinson*

adjective—a word that describes. For example: *tall, narrow, long, flat* (23)

antagonist—a character who opposes the main character (38)

appearance—outward looks. For example: face, hair, body shape, clothes, and ways of movement (23)

believable—true to the story (17)

character—a person or animal in a story (13)

classical hero—strong, courageous, noble-born (37)

climax—the crisis or turning point of the plot (59)

conflict—a problem or struggle between opposing forces (13)

denouement—final wrap up; resolution (59)

description—a word picture which makes use of adjectives and comparisons; written sketch (23)

developing—creating the parts of (26)

dialogue—conversation between characters (66)

dynamic—actively changing or growing; changed by experiences in life (33)

exposition—introduction or beginning of the story (59)

external—outer physical body (33)

falling action—stage after the climax in which the plot winds down (59)

fate—things that happen without an explanation (53)

fiction—a story based on imagination; not a true story (10)

flashback—presentation of earlier events (58)

flat—showing one or few characteristics; vaguely described (30)

flaw—imperfect trait (37)

foil—a character used to set off another character by contrast; character who has opposite traits (38)

functional—filling a specific need (8)

general—inexact (43)

genre—type of fiction (13)

hero—main or central character in a story (37)

heroine—female main or central character in a story (37)

historical people—humans who are living or who have lived (17)

imagery—words or phrases that create pictures in the mind of the reader (72)

in medias res—in the middle of the action (59)

internal—inner (33)

limited—less than complete (67)

literature—writing that has artistic value (1)

lyric—words with a sense of melody (10)

main theme—idea emphasized more than others (62)

mental picture—image in the readers' minds (23)

metaphor—comparison that does not use *like* or *as* (73)

minor theme—lesser or secondary theme (62)

narrative—writing that tells a story (10)

narrator—person telling a story (66)

nature—Earth's forces (53)

nonfiction—writing based on facts; stories that are actual and true to life (10)

novel—a book-length story (1)

omniscient—all-knowing (68)

personal—meaningful only to one person (8)

personality—typical patterns of behavior and thinking (26)

philosophy—basic ideas about life (8)

place—location where the story happens (17)

play—story written to be acted (1)

plot—a series of planned, related events in a story (13)

poem—a piece of writing that uses verses or stanzas (1)

poetry—writing done in groups of lines (10)

point of view—angle from which the story is told (66)

popular fiction—stories written just for fun (1)

prose—writing done in sentences and paragraphs (10)

protagonist—the main character in a work of fiction; can be male or female; can be good or evil (38)

psychology—study of the way people think, feel, and behave (7)

realistic—actual, up front, true-to-life (7)

relative—based on the other characters; in relation to others (31)

rising action—presentation of details in a story; complication of a story (59)

round—well-developed; showing many characteristics; described in detail (30)

scenery—background items (43)

setting—the place and time of a story (13)

short story—a tale told in a few pages (1)

simile—comparison that uses *like* or *as* (73)

society—group of people with common interests (53)

sociology—the study of people living together in groups (7)

specific—exact (43)

static—not changing or growing; remaining the same (33)

straightforward—direct (27)

structure—the planned order or arrangement in which events happen in a story (18)

style—the individual way authors use or arrange words to express their ideas (66)

sub-plot—minor story line (13)

symbol—a word or object which stands for something other than what it actually is (8)

theme—the main idea of a story (13, 62)

time—point at which the story takes place (17)

tragic hero—main character who is wonderful and yet imperfect in some way (37)

universal—understood the same by everybody (8)

villain—opposes the hero (53)